My Hot Dog Went Out, Can I Have Another?

Other FoxTrot Books by Bill Amend

FoxTrot • Pass the Loot • Black Bart Says Draw • Eight Yards, Down and Out
Bury My Heart at Fun-Fun Mountain • Say Hello to Cactus Flats • May the Force Be with Us, Please
Take Us to Your Mall • The Return of the Lone Iguana • At Least This Place Sells T-shirts
Come Closer, Roger, There's a Mosquito on Your Nose • Welcome to Jasorassic Park
I'm Flying, Jack . . . I Mean, Roger • Think iFruity • Death by Field Trip
Encyclopedias Brown and White • His Code Name Was The Fox
Your Momma Thinks Square Roots Are Vegetables • Who's Up for Some Bonding?
Am I a Mutant or What! • Orlando Bloom Has Ruined Everything

Anthologies

FoxTrot: The Works • FoxTrot *en masse* • Enormously FoxTrot • Wildly FoxTrot
FoxTrot Beyond a Doubt • Camp FoxTrot • Assorted FoxTrot • FoxTrot: Assembled with Care
FoxTrotius Maximus

My Hot Dog Went Out, Can I Have Another?

A FoxTrot Collection
by Bill Amend

Andrews McMeel Publishing
Kansas City

FoxTrot is distributed internationally by Universal Press Syndicate.

05 06 07 08 09 10 BBG 10 9 8 7 6 5 4 3 2 1

ISBN-13: 978-0-7407-5441-8
ISBN-10: 0-7407-5441-6

Library of Congress Control Number: 2005925091

www.andrewsmcmeel.com

ATTENTION: SCHOOLS AND BUSINESSES

Andrews McMeel books are available at quantity discounts with bulk purchase for educational, business, or sales promotional use. For information, please write to: Special Sales Department, Andrews McMeel Publishing, 4520 Main Street, Kansas City, Missouri 64111.

WHATCHA PLAYING?
IT'S THE "EXTREME MAKEOVER" HOME EDITION.

YOU SCAN IN PHOTOS OF PEOPLE AND PERFORM PLASTIC SURGERIES TO MAKE THEM LOOK BETTER.
AMEND

I SEE YOU'VE STARTED WITH YOURSELF.
HEY, WE CAN ALL USE A LITTLE IMPROVE-MENT.

VIRTUAL PLASTIC SURGERY. WHAT WILL THEY THINK OF NEXT?
WANT TO TRY ONE?

I'LL SCAN IN A PICTURE OF MOM SO YOU CAN MESS WITH HER.
AMEND

HELLOOO, DOLLY PARTON!

BETTER LOCK THE DOOR, SON.
...BEFORE SHE MESSES WITH YOU.

JASON, THIS "EXTREME MAKEOVER" SOFTWARE IS GREAT!
AMEND

I'VE DONE ABOUT EIGHT COSMETIC SURGERIES ON YOUR MOTHER AND LOOK AT THE RESULTS!

SHE'S A TOTAL KNOCKOUT NOW!

"NOW"?!
...NOW AS ALWAYS?

YOU GAVE ME A VIRTUAL "EXTREME MAKEOVER"?!
JUST FOR LAUGHS.

YOU REALLY THINK I LOOK BETTER LIKE THIS? WITH A QUADRUPLE-D CHEST AND A NOSE JOB?!

ACTUALLY, THE TUMMY TUCK MADE THE BIGGEST DIFFERENCE.

YOUR MOTHER HAS NO SENSE OF HUMOR.
NICE LOOK.
SPORTY BOY
AMEND

ANDY, SWEETIE, I WAS JUST GOOFING AROUND WITH THAT MAKEOVER SOFTWARE. YOU KNOW I LOVE YOU EXACTLY THE WAY YOU ARE.

I DON'T WANT SOME DROP-DEAD GORGEOUS, HOT-BODIED WIFE!
AMEND

I'M NOT HELPING MYSELF RIGHT NOW, AM I?
CAN YOU SAY "FREE FALL"?

WHAT ARE YOU DOING?
GIVING YOU A TASTE OF YOUR OWN VIRTUAL MAKEOVER MEDICINE.

IF IT'S ALL RIGHT FOR YOU TO IMAGINE ME WITH AN IDEALIZED NEW FACE AND BODY, THEN I SHOULD BE ALLOWED TO DO THE SAME THING WITH YOU.
AMEND

TAKE A LOOK. **NOW** HOW DO YOU FEEL? EMBARRASSED? HUMILIATED? FLAWED?

THAT LOOKS JUST LIKE ME. WHAT'D YOU CHANGE?
THAT'S VIGGO MORTENSEN, YOU NUMBSKULL!

HEY, WHAT'S UP?
DID YOU GET THAT FILE I SENT?

I DID INDEED.
WHAT'D YOU THINK?

THUMBS UP ALL THE WAY.
I THOUGHT YOU'D LIKE IT.

CHECK OUT MY NEW WATCH.
COOL. I LIKE THE COLOR.

SOMEONE'S COMING. I SHOULD PROBABLY GO.
OK. SEE YA.
AMEND

A
VIDEO-CONFERENC-ING ON THE CHEAP.
I FORGOT TO ASK YOU SOMETHING. ARE YOU STILL THERE?

WHERE'S JASON?
AT THE POST OFFICE MAILING HIS RESUME.

TO WHOM?!
HE'S DECIDED TO APPLY FOR THE CEO JOB AT DISNEY, JUST IN CASE MICHAEL EISNER GETS THE BOOT.

YOU'VE GOT TO BE KID-DING ME.
HE CLAIMS HE'S COME UP WITH SOME INNOVATIVE WAYS TO IMPROVE THINGS.

I SAID I WANT REAL GHOSTS IN THE HAUNTED MANSION!
YES, SIR, MR. FOX, SIR!
AMEND

SO JASON HAS GOOD IDEAS FOR THE DISNEY COMPANY?
I NEVER SAID THE WORD "GOOD."
SPORTY

WE DIG, DIG, DIG, DIG, DIG, DIG, DIG IN OUR MINE, THE WHOLE DAY THROUGH...
BALROG!
AMEND

DARE I ASK WHAT OTHER CHANGES JASON WOULD BRING TO DISNEY?
HE MENTIONED UPDATING SOME OF THE MOVIES.
SPORTY
AMEND

The Fox and the Hound

Beauty and the Beast

DUMBO

I ALWAYS THOUGHT JASON PREFERRED JAPANESE ANIMATION.
MAYBE HE FIGURES AS DISNEY CEO, HE CAN CHANGE THINGS.
SPORTY

THAT MUSIC YOU ARE PLAYING SOUNDS LIKE "TURKEY IN THE STRAW"! I MUST SAY IT IS CATCHY!
IT IS "TURKEY IN THE STRAW"! WHO KNEW THAT GOATS MADE SUCH GOOD VICTROLAS?! I CERTAINLY DIDN'T!
AMEND

JASON ISN'T EVEN OLD ENOUGH TO SEE SOME DISNEY-OWNED MOVIES!
MAYBE AS CEO HE'LL HAVE THEM TAMED DOWN.
SPORTY

YOU KNOW WHAT THEY CALL A WATER BUFFALO WITH CHEESE IN THE PRIDELANDS?
THEY DON'T CALL IT A WATER BUFFALO WITH CHEESE?
AMEND

YOU DIDN'T MAIL YOUR RESUME?
I DECIDED AGAINST IT AT THE LAST MINUTE.

DISNEY IS A HUGE CORPORATION. I GOT SCARED THAT RUNNING THE COMPANY MIGHT REQUIRE A LOT OF WORK.
AMEND

DUH. WHAT'D YOU EXPECT?!
WELL...

I DON'T HAVE TO GET OFF! I'M THE CEO!
BUT SIR, YOU'VE BEEN RIDING IT FOR A WEEK...
SPACE MOUNTAIN

WAS SOMEONE PLAYING DARTS IN THE LIVING ROOM?!?
IT'S LIKE SHE'S PSYCHIC.
I'LL BET PAIGE RATTED ON US.
IT'S BEEN NICE KNOWING YOU BOYS.
AMEND

PETER, DO YOU NEED ME TO WASH YOUR BASEBALL UNIFORM?
NO.
AMEND

WHAT ABOUT YOUR PRACTICE UNIFORM?
NO.

YOU'RE SURE? THEY DON'T HAVE GRASS OR SWEAT STAINS OR RUBBED-IN DIRT?
I TOLD YOU NO!

IT'S SO NICE HAVING A BENCH-WARMER FOR A SON.
SPEAK-ING OF HAVING THINGS RUBBED IN...

WHAT ARE YOU DOING?
GETTING THE SOLES OF MY BOOTS READY FOR THE RAINY SEASON.
AMEND

BY WATERPROOFING THEM OR SOMETHING?
OR SOMETHING.
CAULK

SPLISH
SPLOSH
SPLISH
SPLOSH
Jason
is great
Jason
is great
Jason

I THINK THE BLOCK-BUSTER SUCCESS OF THIS MEL GIBSON "PASSION" MOVIE IS A GOOD THING.
HOLLYWOOD IS A BUNCH OF COPYCATS, AND I FOR ONE WOULD LOVE TO SEE ISSUES OF FAITH AND RELIGION REFLECTED MORE IN OUR POPULAR CULTURE.
AMEND

COMING THIS SUMMER: "ALIEN VERSUS PREDATOR VERSUS JESUS," RATED R!

BE CAREFUL WHAT YOU WISH FOR.
MAYBE "LOVE" WAS TOO STRONG A WORD.

HA! I WIN!
NO YOU DON'T.

YES I DO! SCISSORS BEATS PAPER!
THIS ISN'T PAPER.

IT'S A SHEET OF MILITARY-GRADE HARDENED STEEL. MILITARY-GRADE HARDENED STEEL BEATS SCISSORS EVERY TIME.
AMEND

MEANWHILE, PAIGE BEATS JASON...
OK, OK, I'LL GIVE YOU ANOTHER CHANCE.

AMEND

CRASH!

WHAT DID YOU DO NOW?!
YOU SAID THE COMPUTER NEEDED BACKING UP!

THERE'S GOT TO BE AT LEAST A FEW IN HERE SOMEWHERE!

RIGHT?! RIGHT?! EVERY GAME HAS THEM!
AMEND

SECRET LEVELS OR SECRET CUTSCENES OR SECRET WEAPONS OR GOOFY MESSAGES THE PROGRAMMERS SNUCK IN! WHERE ARE THEY?! I'VE LOOKED EVERYWHERE!

MOST KIDS HUNT FOR NORMAL EASTER EGGS, JASON.
WHAT ARE THOSE?

HA HA! I GOT ONE MORE MARSHMALLOW CHICK THAN YOU!
THAT'S OK.

I DON'T REALLY LIKE THOSE MARSHMALLOW CHICKS.

HA HA! YOU GOT ONE MORE MARSHMALLOW CHICK THAN ME!
AMEND

MMM.
WHAT KIND OF SANDWICH IS THAT?

PEANUT BUTTER EGG AND JELLYBEAN.
AMEND

THE WEEK AFTER EASTER SO ROCKS.
I NEED TO START MAKING **MY** LUNCHES.

AAAA! I'M LATE FOR SCHOOL!
AMEND

PAIGE, YOU STILL HAVE SHAMPOO IN YOUR HAIR!
I'LL RINSE IT ON THE WAY!

SPRING HAS ITS PLUSSES.

IF THE AMOUNT SHOWN ON LINE 31 IS LESS THAN THE AMOUNT ON LINE 24c...

CONSULT IRS PUBLICATION 5328-7: "LEARN TO ADD, YOU BONEHEAD."

I THINK YOUR EVIL TWIN HAS TAKEN A JOB WITH THE GOVERNMENT.
THAT SOUNDS MORE LIKE MY POLITE TWIN.
AMEND

STAR LIGHT, STAR BRIGHT, FIRST STAR I SEE TONIGHT...
AMEND

I WISH I MAY, I WISH I MIGHT, HAVE THE WISH I WISH TONIGHT.

THAT'S NOT A STAR. IT'S VENUS.

PLANET LIGHT, PLANET BRIGHT...

I ALWAYS FORGET... IS IT "IE" OR "EI"?...

DADDY, HOW DO YOU SPELL "RELIEF"?
R-O-L-A-I-D-S.
AMEND

AND I THOUGHT MY SPELLING WAS BAD.

PUT SOME MORE OH⁻ IONS ON IT.
WE TAKE OUR BASEBALL LITERALLY.
A
AMEND

"NATURE ABHORS A VACUUM," MY FANNY.
I THOUGHT FOR SURE WE'D AT LEAST SEE A FEW LIGHTNING STRIKES.
AMEND

I'M THINKING OF DRAGGING YOUR FATHER TO A MOVIE TONIGHT.
GO SEE "KILL BILL - VOLUME 2." IT'S AWESOME.

REALLY AWESOME. AMAZINGLY AWESOME.

HOW WOULD YOU KNOW? IT'S RATED R.
UM...
SPORTYBOY

THEN AGAIN, MAYBE WE SHOULD STAY HOME FOR "KILL PETER."
NO, NO, DON'T LET ME STOP YOU.
AMEND

I'M GROUNDED FOR A WEEK?! JUST FOR SEEING "KILL BILL - VOLUME 2"?!
UNTIL YOU'RE 17, THAT SORT OF FILM IS TABOO, PETER.

YOU DIDN'T GET UPSET WHEN I SAW "KILL BILL - VOLUME 1"!

I DIDN'T **KNOW** YOU SAW "KILL BILL - VOLUME 1."
AMEND

THIS IS GOING FROM BAD TO WORSE, ISN'T IT?
TWO WEEKS.

I CAN'T BE-LIEVE YOU'RE GROUNDING ME FOR TWO WEEKS!
YOU KNOW HOW I FEEL ABOUT R-RATED FILMS, PETER.
AMEND

YOU SHOULD HAVE THOUGHT ABOUT THE CONSEQUENCES BEFORE YOU SAW THE "KILL BILL" MOVIES.

BUT STEVE AND I MADE PLANS FOR THIS FRIDAY NIGHT!
YOU'LL JUST HAVE TO POSTPONE THEM.

BUT "DAWN OF THE DEAD" WON'T BE IN THEATERS MUCH LONGER!

HA! YOU CAN'T GROUND ME!
WHAT ARE YOU TALKING ABOUT?

YOU DIDN'T READ ME MY MIRANDA RIGHTS PRIOR TO MY ADMITTING TO SEEING "KILL BILL"! YOU HAVE NO CASE! MY TWO-WEEK GROUNDING IS NULL AND VOID!

I'M FREE AS A BIRD! SEE YOU LATER!
WOULD YOU LIKE TO BE GROUNDED FOR THREE WEEKS, PETER?

WELCOME BACK TO COURT-TV...
SOME HELP YOU ARE.
AMEND

NO FAIR! PETER SAW BOTH "KILL BILL" MOVIES?!
HE DID.
AMEND

AND NOW HE'S GROUNDED FOR TWO WEEKS.

LET THAT SERVE AS A LESSON TO YOU.

HMM. SO IN THEORY, I COULD SEE THEM WITHOUT ANY REPERCUS-SIONS...
WELL, NO, YOU I'D MAKE **LEAVE** THE HOUSE.

MOM GROUNDED YOU FOR SEEING "KILL BILL"?
YUP.

YOU CAN'T LEAVE THE HOUSE FOR TWO WEEKS?
ONLY FOR SCHOOL.
AMEND

HA! HA!
CAREFUL. HE THROWS THINGS.

I'M SUPPOSED TO GO WORK OUT TODAY.
GOOD LUCK.
AND PLANT FLOWERS.
GOOD LUCK.
AMEND
AND DO THE GROCERY SHOPPING.
GOOD LUCK.
AND DO THE KIDS' LAUNDRY.
GOOD LUCK.
I PICKED UP A PENNY.
SO, HOW'D YOU HURT YOUR BACK, ANYWAY?

MOM, YOU CAN'T GROUND ME FOR 14 DAYS...IT'S TOO LONG!

I WON'T MAKE IT! I WON'T SURVIVE! I WASN'T MADE TO SPEND THAT MUCH TIME AT HOME!

PLEASE RECONSIDER THE LENGTH! PLEASE! PLEASE! PLEASE!
AMEND

HOW MANY DAYS DO **YOU** THINK IS SUFFICIENT PUNISHMENT?
I WAS THINKING MORE IN TERMS OF MINUTES.
WANNA PLAY D&D?

HEY, PETER— WOULD YOU MIND INSTALLING THIS RAM MODULE INTO THE COMPUTER?
WHY ME?

BECAUSE MOM SAYS YOU'RE GROUNDED.
AMEND

WAAAA HA HA HA HA HA HA!

THAT JOKE ALWAYS KILLS ME.
OR NEARLY.

RING!
RING!
RING!

HEY, PETE, IT'S STEVE. MY COUSIN THE PARISIAN SWIMSUIT MODEL IS IN TOWN AND SHE HAS AN EXTRA FRONT-ROW TICKET TO SEE METALLICA. YOU FREE THIS WEEKEND?

SLAM!
AMEND

RING!
RING!
RING!
I SHOULD NEVER HAVE TOLD PEOPLE I WAS GROUNDED.

DO YOU KNOW WHAT THE WEATHER IS SUPPOSED TO BE LIKE TOMORROW?
AWFUL.

LOUSY.

THE WORST WEATHER POSSIBLE.
AMEND

I'LL TAKE THAT TO MEAN WARM AND SUNNY.
I HATE BEING GROUNDED.

GOT A SECOND?
WHAT FOR?

I KNOW I TOLD YOU YOU WERE GROUNDED FOR TWO WEEKS, PETER, BUT I THINK I'M GOING TO LET YOU OFF AFTER ONE.
WOOHOO! HOW COME?

I'VE DECIDED KEEPING YOU IN THE HOUSE THAT LONG IS TOO CRUEL A PUNISHMENT.
THAT'S WHAT I'VE BEEN SAYING SINCE DAY ONE!
AMEND

I MEANT FOR THE REST OF US.
I FIGURED OUT HOW TO BURP THE ESPN THEME. WANNA HEAR?

ANY FINAL THOUGHTS ON HOW PETER'S PUNISHMENT WENT?
IT'S INTERESTING.
GOLFSTER

THE WHOLE TIME HE WAS GROUNDED HIS HOMEWORK GOT DONE, HIS ROOM GOT CLEANED, AND HE WENT TO BED AT A DECENT HOUR EACH NIGHT.
AMEND

IT HAS ME A LITTLE WORRIED.
GOLFSTER

ABOUT WHAT?
I THINK I WANT HIM TO GET IN TROUBLE MORE OFTEN.
GOLFSTER

LET'S JUST ASSUME IT'LL END UP A GUTTER BALL.
I WAS HOW OLD WHEN WE STARTED?
AMEND

I'M BORED.

TOTALLY BORED.

PAINFULLY, HEAD-READY-TO-EXPLODE, UNBELIEVABLY BORED.

YOU COULD HELP ME IN THE GARDEN.
I'M KINDA BUSY COMPLAINING RIGHT NOW, THANKS.
AMEND

DO ME A FAVOR AND BREAK UP THE SOIL WITH THIS SHOVEL.
I CAN'T DO THAT!

THAT SHOVEL IS TOO HEAVY! THE GROUND IS TOO HARD! IT'S TOO MUCH WORK!
AMEND

YOU DIG 10-FOOT-DEEP HOLES WITH THIS SHOVEL EVERY OTHER WEEKEND LOOKING FOR PIRATE TREASURE.

MY ARMS ARE TIRED.
DIG!

HERE. SPRINKLE SOME OF THIS ALONG EACH ROW.
WHAT IS IT?

PLANT FOOD.
AMEND

IT'LL HELP MAKE THE VEGETABLES BIG AND TASTY.

WHAT'S NEEDED IS A PRODUCT TO MAKE THEM TINY AND FLAVORLESS.

WHAT ARE YOU DOING?
PICKING OUT ALL THE EARTH-WORMS.

I ASSUME YOU DON'T WANT THEM IN WITH THE VEGETABLES.
AMEND

NONSENSE. WORMS ARE GOOD FOR THE SOIL. PUT THEM ALL BACK.

WHERE ARE YOU GOING?
I UM, LEFT SOME THINGS IN PAIGE'S SOCK DRAWER.

DRIP...
PEAS

DRIP...
SPINACH
AMEND

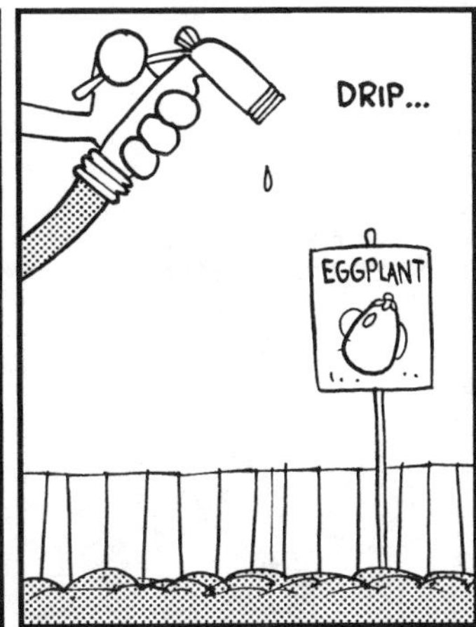
DRIP...
EGGPLANT

IF YOU DON'T WATER THEM ENOUGH, THEY WON'T GROW, JASON.
SHE'S ON TO ME.

THANKS FOR ALL THE HELP IN THE GARDEN, JASON.

YOU DUG... YOU PLANTED... YOU WATERED...
AMEND

I DO BELIEVE I SEE THE BEGINNINGS OF A GREEN THUMB!

YOU AREN'T TURNING INTO THE HULK, JASON.
SAYS YOU.
A
GUYS LIFE

What is the capital of Mexico?

Answer:
Quebec

$\sqrt{9} = ?$

Answer:
Negative infinity

In the U.S., what are the three branches of government?

Answer:
Larry, Moe and Curly

WHAT ARE YOU DOING?
GETTING READY FOR FINAL EXAMS.

I'M SO PROUD OF YOU, PAIGE! AND I DIDN'T EVEN HAVE TO NAG!

SHOULD I LEAVE MY TENNIS RACQUET TO PETER, SINCE YOU ALREADY HAVE ONE?
AMEND

YOU'RE WRITING YOUR **WILL**?!
HOW DO **YOU** PREPARE FOR TESTS?

I'VE NEVER UNDERSTOOD THE TECHNOLOGY BEHIND NASCAR.
A
Mr. CHIPS

HOW DO THEY GET THOSE BILLBOARDS TO ZOOM AROUND THE TRACK LIKE THAT?
AMEND

A

THOSE AREN'T BILLBOARDS. THEY'RE CARS.
AND HOW DO THOSE HUMAN-SHAPED BILLBOARDS STEER THEM?
A

CAN YOU NAME ONE PERSON DUMBER THAN PAIGE?
AMEND

CAN YOU NAME ONE PERSON UGLIER THAN PAIGE?

CAN YOU NAME ONE PERSON WITH WORSE BREATH THAN PAIGE?

CAN HE NAME ONE PERSON DEADER THAN JASON?
HEY, IT'S QUINCY WHO'S INSULTING YOU!

THIS IS MY F-CHORD...
A

THIS IS MY G-CHORD...

THIS IS MY H-CHORD...
I DIDN'T KNOW THERE **WERE** H-CHORDS.
A

HE SAYS ROCK AND ROLL IS ALL ABOUT REBELLION.
SO IS THE H FOR "HORRIBLE" OR "HIDEOUS"?
AMEND

IT WAS FOUNDED IN 1994 AND WENT ONLINE IN 1995.

IT SHIPPED ITS ONE MILLIONTH BOOK IN 1997 AND REPORTED ITS FIRST PROFITABLE QUARTER IN JANUARY 2002.
AMEND

ITS CEO IS JEFF BEZOS AND IT IS BASED IN SEATTLE, WASHINGTON.

YOUR ASSIGNED SUBJECT WAS THE AMAZON **RIVER**, JASON.
I CHECKED —THEY DON'T OWN A RIVER.

DO WE HAVE ANY ASPIRIN?
THERE'S SOME IN THE KITCHEN CUPBOARD. WHAT'S WRONG?
THYME

I HURT MY THIGH PLAYING GOLF.

BECAUSE YOU FORGOT TO STRETCH BEFOREHAND?
AMEND
Herb Alpert Presents...
THYME

BECAUSE I BROKE MY 4-IRON OVER MY LEG.
YOU'D THINK I'D LEARN.
THYME

GOTCHA!
GOTCHA!

GOTCHA!
GOTCHA!

GOTCHA!
GOTCHA!

SHOW-OFF!

YOU LOOK HAPPY.
YOU BET. IT'S FRESHMAN FAIR DAY.

THE WHOLE FRESHMAN CLASS GETS TO GO TO THE FAIR FOR A BIG END-OF-THE-YEAR FIELD TRIP!
AMEND

IT'S FRESHMAN-FREE DAY! IT'S FRESHMAN-FREE DAY!
PETER SEEMS HAPPY, TOO.
"FAIR," PETER! FRESHMAN FAIR!

OK, FRESHMEN, THE FAIRGROUNDS ARE ALL YOURS. JUST BE BACK ON THE BUSES BY 2:15.

MAYBE WE SHOULD HOLD OUR TRACK MEETS HERE.
WHO'S WEARING SIZE SEVEN REEBOKS?!
AMEND

I ALWAYS HAVE TROUBLE CHOOSING BETWEEN CANDY APPLES AND CARAMEL ONES.
ME TOO.

I FEEL SO SORRY FOR DECISIVE PEOPLE.
I HEAR THE ICE CREAM STAND HAS 14 FLAVORS.
AMEND

ANY CHANCE I COULD INTEREST YOU IN A RIDE ON THE TUNNEL OF LOVE?
THE TUNNEL OF LOVE?!
AMEND

MORTON, LET ME PUT THIS MILDLY: I LOATHE YOU. OK?! L-O-A-T-H-E.

The TUNNEL of LOATHE
THIS FAIR HAS TOO MANY RIDES.
SCOOT CLOSER. I PROBABLY WON'T BITE.

THINK HUNKY BOBBY ROMER SAW ME SITTING ACROSS FROM HIM ON THE SWIRL-O-WHIRL?
I'LL BET HE DID.

YESSS! I'VE BEEN TRYING TO GET HIM TO NOTICE ME ALL YEAR!

THINK HE NOTICED WHEN I PUKED?
DWELL ON THE POSITIVES, PAIGE.
AMEND

HOW WAS THE FAIR?
NOT GREAT, NOT AWFUL.
SMARTO

FAIR?
THAT'S A FAIR ASSESSMENT.

HOW'D THAT NEW SUNSCREEN WORK OUT?
GOOD. STILL FAIR.
SMARTO
AMEND

HEY, THIS PROBLEM IS SUPER EASY!

SO IS THIS ONE!
AND THIS ONE!
AND THIS ONE!

I DON'T SEE A SINGLE ONE I CAN'T DO!

I'M ACING MY MATH FINAL! I'M ACING MY MATH FINAL!

JASON, WILL YOU KEEP IT DOWN?
"JASON"?
AMEND

AAAAAAA!

DO YOU EVER HAVE NIGHTMARES WHERE YOU DO WELL AT SCHOOL?
YOU MEAN LIKE MERELY WELL?

DID YOU FINISH ALL THE READING FOR YOUR ENGLISH FINAL?
NOT REALLY.

PETER!
RELAX. I STILL HAVE TIME LEFT.

WHEN'S THE TEST?
IN 45 MINUTES.
AMEND

AND I THOUGHT "DOOM" WAS A VIDEO GAME.
TOLSTOY IS EASY TO SKIM, RIGHT?

WHAT ARE YOU DOING?
LISTENING TO MOZART AND DRINKING GINKGO-INFUSED SODAS.

I HAVE MY PHYSICS FINAL TOMORROW AND I NEED EVERY ADVANTAGE I CAN MUSTER WHILE I STUDY.
AMEND

SUPPOSEDLY MOZART HELPS WITH MATH SKILLS AND THE GINKGO HELPS WITH MEMORY.

REMEMBERING YOUR TEXTBOOK MIGHT HELP, ALSO.
SEE? THIS IS WHY I NEED THE GINKGO.

YOU'LL BE GRADING THIS TEST ON A CURVE, RIGHT?
TO A CERTAIN EXTENT.

SO, FOR INSTANCE, GETTING 15 OUT OF 20 RIGHT MIGHT STILL BE AN "A"?
IT'S POSSIBLE.
AMEND

DON'T WORRY ABOUT THE CURVE NOW...YOU JUST STARTED.
PHEW.

IT'S JUST THAT THESE FIRST FIVE QUESTIONS HAVE ME STUMPED.
WORRY ABOUT THE CURVE.

DO YOU HAVE ANY CHAPSTICK?
WHAT FOR?

THIS LAST WEEK OF SCHOOL FOR ME HAS BEEN ONE TEARFUL GOODBYE AFTER ANOTHER.
AMEND

MY LIPS ARE WORN OUT FROM ALL THE KISSING.
ARE WE TALKING ABOUT GIRLS, HERE?

MATH BOOKS.
YOU HAD ME WORRIED ABOUT YOU FOR A SECOND THERE.

SO WHAT'LL YOU BE DOING THIS SUMMER, DR. TING?
I'M GLAD YOU ASKED, PAIGE.

I'VE LINED UP A JOB FLIPPING BURGERS AT A FAST-FOOD RESTAURANT.
AMEND

FINALLY, THIS TEACHER'S GONNA KNOW WHAT IT'S LIKE TO EARN SOME SERIOUS MONEY!

HAR HAR. MISS CHRISTOPHER TOLD THE SAME JOKE IN ENGLISH CLASS.
JOKE?

THE NATIONAL CARTOONISTS SOCIETY IS HOLDING ITS ANNUAL REUBEN AWARDS TONIGHT.

BLACK TIE... LIVE MUSIC... PEOPLE FLYING IN FROM ALL OVER THE WORLD TO ATTEND...
AMEND

I GUESS THEY REALLY TAKE THEIR SANDWICHES SERIOUSLY.
MUST BE THE DAGWOOD BUMSTEAD INFLUENCE.

WHAT AN ABSOLUTELY PERFECT SPRING DAY!
I USED TO LOVE WEATHER LIKE THIS BACK IN COLLEGE.
MY BUDDIES AND I WOULD SPEND ENTIRE DAYS LOUNGING AROUND, THROWING FRISBEES ON THE QUAD.
AH, THOSE WERE SOME GOOD TIMES.
SO YOU SKIPPED YOUR CLASSES?
AMEND
UM...
DID YOU KNOW THAT WHEN DAD WAS IN COLLEGE, THE ONLY WARM DAYS WERE ON WEEKENDS?
THAT WAS BACK IN THE ICE AGE, REMEMBER.

HAVE A GREAT TIME AT THE POOL, PAIGE.
"**GREAT**"?!

NEED I REMIND YOU, MOTHER, THAT I'M GOING WITH JASON?
AMEND

A "GREAT TIME" IS SIMPLY NOT POSSIBLE.

HAVE A TOLERABLE TIME AT THE POOL, THEN?
"**TOLER-ABLE**"?!
READY TO GO?

CHECK IT OUT! I CAN TOUCH THE BOTTOM WITH MY FEET!

I COULDN'T DO THIS LAST SUMMER! I MUST BE GETTING TALLER!

WOOHOO! LOOK AT ME! I'M A HUMAN SEQUOIA!

JASON, THAT'S THE KIDDIE POOL.
EVEN SEQUOIAS HAVE TO START SOMEWHERE.
AMEND

MARCO!
RALPH LAUREN!

MARCO!
RALPH LAUREN!

MARCO!
RALPH LAUREN!

YOU KNOW, YOU'RE SUPPOSED TO SAY "POLO," PAIGE.
WHAT'S THE DIFFER-ENCE?
AMEND

HOW LONG CAN YOU HOLD YOUR BREATH UNDER WATER?
52 SECONDS.

I DON'T BELIEVE YOU.
WATCH. I'LL PROVE IT.
AMEND

GLUB
GLUB
GLUB

NOW IF I CAN JUST GET HIM TO DO THIS 130 MORE TIMES, IT'LL BE A PLEASANT AFTERNOON...

DOESN'T THAT BOY OVER THERE GO TO YOUR SCHOOL?
YES. AND IF YOU SAY ANYTHING TO EMBARRASS ME, YOU'RE DEAD.
Verlon
GLAM

BOY, PAIGE, THAT BATHING SUIT SURE DOES A GOOD JOB OF HIDING YOUR CHEST HAIR!

WHAT?? I DIDN'T SAY IT. I SHOUTED IT.
Verlon
GLAM

NEXT BIRTHDAY I'M BUYING HER A DICTIONARY.
AMEND

WHAT'S WRONG?
OUCH! MY BACK!

I GOT REALLY SUNBURNED AT THE POOL TODAY.
DIDN'T YOU PUT ON SUN-SCREEN?
AMEND

YEAH, BUT I COULDN'T REACH MY BACK.
WHY DIDN'T YOU ASK YOUR SISTER TO RUB IT ON YOU?

THERE ARE AGONIES WORSE THAN SUNBURN, MOTHER.
HON-ESTLY, JASON.
OUCH! MY BACK!

GOT ANY GOALS FOR SUMMER VACATION?
ALL I KNOW IS I DON'T WANT A REPEAT OF LAST YEAR'S.
I SPENT EIGHT HOURS A DAY SITTING INSIDE PLAYING VIDEO GAMES.
THAT'S PRETTY PATHETIC.
TELL ME ABOUT IT.
AMEND
I CAN USUALLY GET IN A GOOD 12 HOURS A DAY.
YOUR MOM WORKS OUTSIDE THE HOUSE, THOUGH.
JASON, I SAID TURN THAT OFF!

WHY ARE YOU SO HAPPY?
THE MOVIE THEATER HIRED ME BACK FOR THE SUMMER.

I THOUGHT YOU HATED WORKING THERE.
I GOT A NEW GIG. I'M GOING TO BE THE "SPECIAL PROMOTIONS OPERATIVE."

WHAT'S THAT MEAN?
I'M NOT SURE. BUT IT'S GOT TO BE BETTER THAN LAST YEAR'S STINT AS RESTROOM-MOPPER.
AMEND

ARE YOU SURE YOU DON'T WANT ME MOPPING RESTROOMS?
I KNEW IT! A PERFECT FIT!
SEE MY MOVIE

I HAVE TO WEAR THIS EVERY DAY?!
JUST FOR A WEEK.
SEE MY MOVIE

THE "GARFIELD" MOVIE OPENS FRIDAY AND THE PAVILIONPLEX HOME OFFICE THOUGHT THIS WOULD BE A GOOD WAY TO RAISE AWARENESS.
AMEND

ISN'T THERE SOME OTHER MOVIE I COULD PROMOTE?
THEY DID SEND OVER A "STEPFORD WIVES" COSTUME.
SEE MY MOVIE

I HATE THIS JOB.
THE LINE IS "I HATE MONDAYS," PETER. "MONNN-DAYYYS."
SEE MY MOVIE

ZZZZ...
SEE MY MOVIE

ZZZZ...
SEE MY MOVIE

ZZZZ...
EXCELLENT NAPPING, PETER! EXCELLENT!
SEE MY MOVIE

PLAYING GARFIELD DOES HAVE ONE PERK.
KEEP UP THE GOOD WORK!
SEE MY MOVIE

I SWEAR, IF ONE MORE "GARFIELD" FAN STARTS TALKING TO ME, I'M QUITTING.
SEE MY MOVIE
AMEND

"OHMYGOSH! I'M YOUR BIGGEST FAN!"... "HOW'S ODIE?"... "SAY HI TO JON!" I'M JUST A GUY IN A COSTUME, PEOPLE!

OHMYGOSH! I'M YOUR BIGGEST FAN!
SEE MY MOVIE

MAKE THAT TWO MORE...
HOW'S ODIE?
SEE MY MOVIE

NO OFFENSE, BUT YOU'RE ONE LAME GARFIELD.
THANKS, KID.

SERIOUSLY, YOU DON'T WALK LIKE GARFIELD... YOU DON'T TALK LIKE GARFIELD...

CAN YOU DO ANYTHING LIKE GARFIELD, AT ALL?
AMEND

UGGH.
ROUGH WEEK?

I'VE HAD TO SPEND THE LAST FIVE DAYS DRESSED UP LIKE GARFIELD, MOTHER. "ROUGH" BARELY BEGINS TO DESCRIBE IT.

THANK GOODNESS IT'S OVER.
UM, I THINK YOU LEFT THE EYES IN.

WHOOPS. THANKS.
JASON SAID YOU REALLY WANTED LASAGNA FOR DINNER...
AMEND

I WANT A NEW DRIVER, BUT CAN'T DECIDE BETWEEN THIS ONE AND THIS ONE.
WE HAVE A DRIVING RANGE OUT BACK — WHY DON'T YOU HIT SOME BALLS WITH THEM?
2-irons at 1-iron prices!!!

BECAUSE THEN I WON'T WANT EITHER ONE.
SAY, DIDN'T I SELL YOU A DRIVER **LAST** YEAR?
2-irons at 1-iron prices!!!
AMEND

BUY CANNED MEAT DIRECT AND $$$SAVE$$$!

IMPROVE YOUR LOVE LIFE WITH CANNED MEAT! CLICK HERE TO LEARN HOW!
AMEND

LOSE POUNDS INSTANTLY WITH THE CANNED MEAT DIET!

SPAM-SPAM.
GREETINGS, FRIEND, I AM IN NEED OF HELP WITH THE TRANSFER OF 40 MILLION CANS OF MEAT FROM MY COUNTRY...

ANY CALLS FROM LANGLEY YET?
LANGLEY?

THE DIRECTOR OF THE CIA IS RESIGNING. I ASSUME THEY'LL BE OFFERING ME THE JOB.
YOU??

IT'S THE CENTRAL INTELLIGENCE AGENCY! NO ONE HAS MORE INTELLIGENCE THAN ME!
THAN I.
AMEND

FINE. I'LL DELEGATE GRAMMAR TO MY ENGLISH STATION CHIEF.
I'LL ADMIT YOU ARE GOOD AT BUGGING PEOPLE...

Y-U-C-K-Y

G-R-O-S-S

B-L-E-C-C-H

I'VE GOT A BAD FEELING ABOUT THIS ALPHABET SOUP MOM MADE.
N-O-T-F-I-T-F-O-R-H-U-M-A-N-C-O-N-S-U-M-P-T-I-O-N
AMEND

AMEND

THEY SHOULD CALL THESE THINGS "CRASHERANGS."
SERIOUSLY, I'VE NEVER HEARD IT BOOM ONCE.

I HOPE YOU MADE YOURSELF A DECENT LUNCH WHILE I WAS OUT.
I DID.

WHAT'D YOU HAVE?
A SANDWICH, AN ORANGE, AND SOME MILK.
AMEND

HALLELUJAH. YOU USUALLY EAT JUNK.

AN ICE-CREAM SANDWICH, AN ORANGE SODA, AND MILK DUDS.
SO I ABBREVIATED.

MISS!
2

MISS!
2

ARGGH!
2

I THOUGHT MOM SAID YOU WERE REALLY **GOOD** AT PUTTERING.
THIS IS PUTT-**ING**, SON.
AMEND

I TOLD YOU THESE WOULD GIVE US THE POOL TO OURSELVES.
BIOHAZARD INCOMING!
EXXON VALDEZ
LEAD
Pb
TOXIC WASTE
AMEND

IS IT OUT YET?
NO.
AMEND

IS IT OUT YET?
NO.

IS IT OUT YET?
STOP ASKING ME!

I GUESS THE BRIGHT SIDE IS BY THE TIME "DOOM 3" DOES COME OUT, I'LL BE OLD ENOUGH TO PLAY IT.

I THINK THE FIREFLIES ARE ON TO US.
YOU HAVE TO FLAP YOUR WINGS, DOOFUS.
AMEND

I EAT OREOS WHOLE. HOW DO YOU EAT THEM?
I TWIST THEM OPEN AND LICK THE INSIDES.

BUT JUST A LITTLE. THEN I PRESS THE HALVES BACK TOGETHER AND RETURN THEM TO THE PACKAGE.

IT'S MORE FUN THAT WAY.

THAT'S DISGUSTING, PAIGE!
AMEND

I TOLD YOU IT WAS TOO HOT OUT FOR SQUIRT GUNS.
MAYBE WE SHOULD TRY IT IN THE SHADE.
AMEND

JASON, YOU'RE GREAT!
JASON, YOU'RE WONDERFUL!
JASON, YOU'RE AMAZING!
WHY AREN'T YOU ASLEEP?
MY FAN'S TOO LOUD.
THYME
AMEND

WORK COMES BEFORE PLEASURE, SON.
NOT ACCORDING TO WEBSTER.
Dictionary
AMEND

THINK PEOPLE WILL SUSPECT THAT WE'RE IN CAHOOTS?
MAYBE I SHOULD MOVE DOWN THE STREET SOME.
Free extra-salty Popcorn
Lemonade $50
AMEND

YAWN.
I HOPE THAT AT LEAST ONCE THIS SUMMER I'LL HAVE OCCASION TO SAY SOMETHING.

WHAT'S THAT?
"GOOD MORNING, PAIGE."

YOU COULD SAY IT WHEN I GO TO BED...
DON'T EAT TOO MUCH CEREAL— DINNER'S IN AN HOUR.
AMEND

A PERFECT DRIVE! 300 YARDS DOWN THE MIDDLE OF THE FAIRWAY!

HOLY COW! WHAT A SECOND SHOT! I'M ON THE PAR-5 GREEN IN TWO!
AMEND

I DRAINED THE 30-FOOT PUTT FOR AN EAGLE! I WON THE TOURNAMENT! I WON THE TOURNAMENT!

I THOUGHT YOU SAID THIS GOLF GAME WAS REALISTIC.
I GUESS THE TREES **DO** LOOK A LITTLE FAKE.
TIGER WANTS A REMATCH.

SHOULD I DRESS LIKE SPIDER-MAN OR DOC OC FOR THE "S-2" OPENING?
EITHER WAY YOU'LL LOOK LIKE THE WORLD'S BIGGEST LOSER.
Fox Mactor
GLAM!
AMEND

ACTUALLY, TO ACHIEVE THAT I'D JUST NEED A T-SHIRT THAT SAYS "PAIGE FOX IS MY SISTER."

I SEE YOU WENT WITH THE SPIDER-MAN COSTUME.
IT HIDES THE BANDAGES BETTER.

3... 2... 1... LIFTOFF!
NASA
AMEND

I THINK THE PAYLOAD WAS TOO TOP-HEAVY.
MAYBE WE SHOULDN'T TRY LAUNCHING BARBIES.

BULL'S-EYE!

BULL'S-EYE!

ANOTHER BULL'S-EYE!

NOW THIS IS A DARTBOARD I CAN LOVE!
AMEND

I'VE BEEN AT THE GYM ALL DAY. CAN YOU TELL?
ABSOLUTELY.
A
FOURTEEN

REALLY?!
IT'S TOTALLY OBVIOUS, PETER.
A
AMEND

WHAT GAVE IT AWAY? MY PECS OR MY BICEPS?
YOUR LACK OF A GOOD DEODORANT.
A
FOURTEEN

HAPPY FOURTH OF JULY!
HAPPY FOURTH OF JULY!
HAPPY FOURTH OF JULY!
THIS MIGHT BE A HAMBURGER. I CAN'T TELL.
MY HOT DOG WENT OUT. CAN I HAVE ANOTHER?

DO WE HAVE A PHILLIPS-HEAD SCREW-DRIVER?
THERE SHOULD BE ONE IN THE TOOLBOX.

WHAT ABOUT A TAPE MEASURE?
I THINK THERE'S ONE IN THE DRAWER WITH THE SCISSORS.
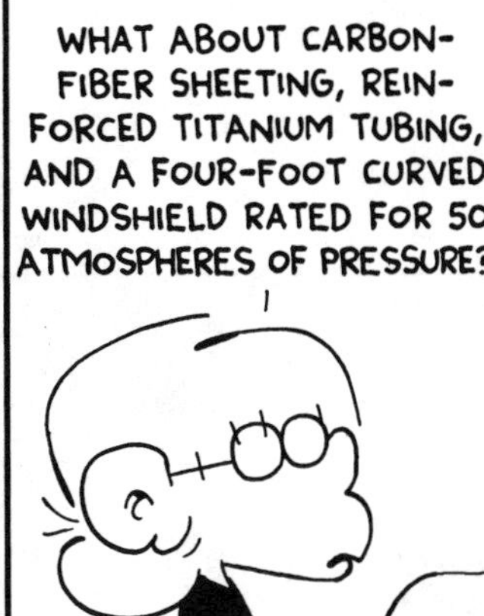
WHAT ABOUT CARBON-FIBER SHEETING, REIN-FORCED TITANIUM TUBING, AND A FOUR-FOOT CURVED WINDSHIELD RATED FOR 50 ATMOSPHERES OF PRESSURE?

IT'S FOR A, UM, "PROJECT."
PERHAPS YOU SHOULD "FIND A NEW ONE."
AMEND

WHAT ARE YOU DOING?
I'M DESIGNING A ROCKET TO WIN THE $10 MILLION X-PRIZE.

ALL IT HAS TO DO IS LIFT THREE PEOPLE INTO SPACE TWICE IN TWO WEEKS. HOW HARD CAN THAT BE?

WANT TO BE ONE OF THE PASSENGERS?

MOM, DO WE HAVE A MEGA-PHONE? I NEED TO LAUGH IN JASON'S FACE LOUDER THAN USUAL.
LOOKS LIKE I'VE DIS-COVERED THE HARD PART.
AMEND

HOW CAN I HELP YOU BOYS?
WE NEED TO BUY SOME MODEL ROCKET ENGINES.
CALVIN'S HOBBIES

HOW MANY?
WHAT'D WE DECIDE ON?
650 THOUSAND.
AMEND

WE CAN PAY YOU IN TWO WEEKS AFTER WE WIN THE $10 MILLION X-PRIZE.
CALVIN'S HOBBIES

BOYS...
WILL YOU ACCEPT A CHARIZARD POKÉMON CARD AS DOWN-PAYMENT?
MINT CON-DITION.
CALVIN'S HOBBIES

IT'S A GOOD THING WE'RE RUNNING WIND-TUNNEL TESTS BEFORE LIFT-OFF.
READY TO CRANK IT UP TO "MEDIUM"?
J+M
J+M Aerospace
AMEND

I'VE WRITTEN A PROGRAM TO SIMULATE THE FLIGHT OF OUR THREE-PERSON ROCKET.
IT'S NOT FLYING.

IT'S STILL NOT FLYING.

IT'S BURSTING INTO FLAMES.

I MUST'VE MESSED UP A LINE OF CODE OR SOMETHING.
IT'S PLAYING "TAPS."
AMEND

HOW GOES THE SPACEFLIGHT BUSINESS?
SADLY, WE'VE GIVEN IT UP.

THE BURT RUTAN GROUP HAS TOO MUCH OF A HEAD START. WE'D NEVER WIN THE $10 MILLION X-PRIZE AT THE RATE WE WERE GOING.

MAYBE SOMEDAY THERE'LL BE A Y-PRIZE WE CAN COMPETE FOR.
AMEND

YOU WON THE "WHY" PRIZE LONG AGO, JASON.
IS IT OK IF WE LEAVE OUR ROCKET IN THE DRIVE-WAY? THE TEST ENGINE SORTA FUSED WITH THE ASPHALT.

HI. CAN I HAVE A FROZEN FRODO?
SORRY. I'M SOLD OUT OF THOSE.

HOW 'BOUT A RAIN-BOW POPALICIOUS, THEN?
I'M OUT OF THOSE, TOO.

AN ARCTIC PIE?
OUT.
A BERRY BLIZZARD?
OUT.
A CHOCO KHAN?
SORRY.

DO YOU HAVE ANYTHING?
LET'S SEE...

NICE ICE CUBE.
NEXT TIME LET ME ORDER FIRST, OK?!
AMEND

WHAT ARE YOU WATCHING?
THE HISTORY CHANNEL.

THEY'RE RUNNING A DOCUMENTARY ON THE AMERICAN REVOLUTION.
AMEND

SOUNDS THRILLING.
WELL, THEY SPICED IT UP A LITTLE.

"FAHRENHEIT 7/4" WILL BE BACK AFTER THESE MESSAGES...
I LOVE THE SHOTS OF CORNWALLIS POWDERING HIS WIG.

FIRE.

BLINDED BY THE LIGHT.
AMEND

BORN TO RUN.

DO YOU SUPPOSE SPRINGSTEEN ONCE SAW DAD TRYING TO LIGHT CHARCOAL?
AAAA! I'M ON FIRE! I'M ON FIRE!

DO YOU HAVE A RED PEN?
WHAT FOR?

I WANT TO MAKE LITTLE RED MARKS ON MY NECK AND CHIN SO THE HOT COLLEGE GIRLS AT THE POOL WILL THINK I CUT MYSELF SHAVING.
AMEND

I DON'T WANT THEM THINKING I'M SOME WIMPY HIGH-SCHOOLER WHO CAN'T GROW FACIAL HAIR.

YOU'D RATHER THEY THINK YOU'RE A WEIRDO HIGH-SCHOOLER WHO CAN'T GROW FACIAL HAIR?
WELL, **PAIGE** SAYS IT'S A GREAT IDEA.

HON, I THINK YOUR TIRES ARE GETTING LOW.
REALLY? I JUST FILLED THEM.

THEY LOOK FINE TO ME.
LET'S TALK ABOUT YOUR DIET, THEN.
AMEND

REMEMBER THE BLASTER WORM THAT CAME OUT ABOUT A YEAR AGO?

THE ONE THAT WOULD CONTINUALLY SHUT DOWN COMPUTERS, OVER AND OVER?
AMEND

LAUNCHING STARCRAFT...

JASON, I SAID TURN THAT THING OFF AND PLAY OUTSIDE!
I HAVE A THEORY ABOUT WHO WROTE IT.

WHAT'S THAT YOU'RE PUTTING ON?
IT'S A SELF-TANNER.

I FIGURE IT'S A LOT SAFER THAN LYING OUT IN THE YARD.
AMEND

THAT'S TRUE. NO NEED TO RISK SKIN CANCER.
WHO'S TALKING ABOUT SKIN CANCER?

THESE NINJA STARS FLY GREAT!
WASN'T YOUR SISTER SUNBATHING OUT HERE A MINUTE AGO?

MAY I TAKE YOUR ORDER?
YES, I'D LIKE A BURGER, FRIES, AND A LARGE ROOT BEER.
DID YOU WANT A BUN WITH YOUR BURGER?
UM, YES...
AND DID YOU WANT POTATO IN YOUR FRENCH FRIES?
HOW ELSE?
DID YOU SAY ROOT BEER? WE DON'T HAVE DIET ROOT BEER.
I MEANT REGULAR ROOT BEER.
AMEND
SYD, I HAVE A HIGH-CARB SPECIAL ORDER COMING THROUGH.
IT MIGHT BE A FEW MINUTES— HE NEEDS TO FIND A BUN.
THIS ATKINS CRAZE CAN'T END SOON ENOUGH.
CAN I EXCHANGE THIS SALAD? IT HAS A CROUTON.

YOU KNOW WHAT I'M IN THE MOOD FOR? HOMEMADE CHOCOLATE CHIP COOKIES.

YUP. FRESH-FROM-THE-OVEN, WARM, DELICIOUS CHOCOLATE CHIP COOKIES.
AMEND

DID I MENTION I'M IN THE MOOD FOR HOMEMADE CHOCOLATE CHIP COOKIES?

ARE YOU SURE YOU AREN'T JUST IN A MOOD TO ANNOY ME?
I CAN BE IN BOTH MOODS AT ONCE, CAN'T I?

WHAT ARE YOU DOING?
MOM WON'T MAKE ME CHOCOLATE CHIP COOKIES, SO I'M MAKING THEM MYSELF.

ARE YOU SURE THAT'S A GOOD IDEA?
WHY WOULDN'T IT BE?

THIS RECIPE CALLS FOR EGGS. DO THEY MEAN CHICKEN EGGS? SNAKE EGGS? FISH EGGS?

CALL IT A HUNCH.
MOM, DO WE HAVE ANY SNAKE EGGS?
AMEND

THIS COOKIE RECIPE CALLS FOR A HALF-TEASPOON OF BAKING SODA.

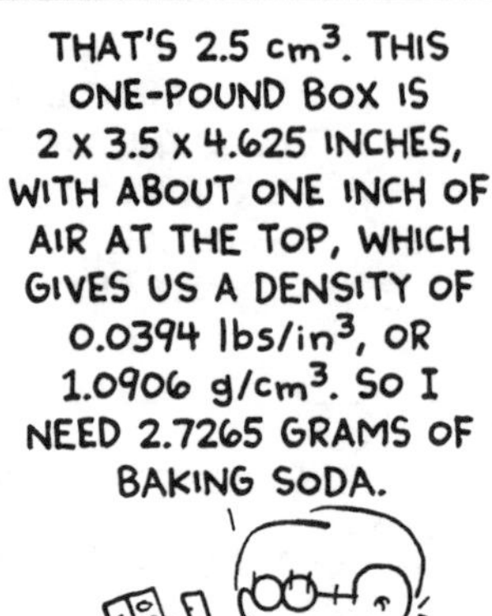
THAT'S 2.5 cm3. THIS ONE-POUND BOX IS 2 x 3.5 x 4.625 INCHES, WITH ABOUT ONE INCH OF AIR AT THE TOP, WHICH GIVES US A DENSITY OF 0.0394 lbs/in3, OR 1.0906 g/cm3. SO I NEED 2.7265 GRAMS OF BAKING SODA.

MOM, DO YOU HAVE A PRECISION METRIC SCALE?
AMEND

WHY DON'T YOU USE THIS HALF-TEASPOON MEASURE INSTEAD?
WHERE'S THE FUN IN THAT?

THE RECIPE SAYS TO BAKE THE COOKIES IN A 350-DEGREE OVEN FOR 14 MINUTES.
AMEND

DO THEY MEAN 350 DEGREES FAHRENHEIT, OR 350 DEGREES CELSIUS?

OR 350 DEGREES KELVIN?

MAYBE THEY WANT YOU TO ROTATE THE OVEN JUST SHY OF A FULL CIRCLE.
DON'T BE RIDICU-LOUS, PETER.

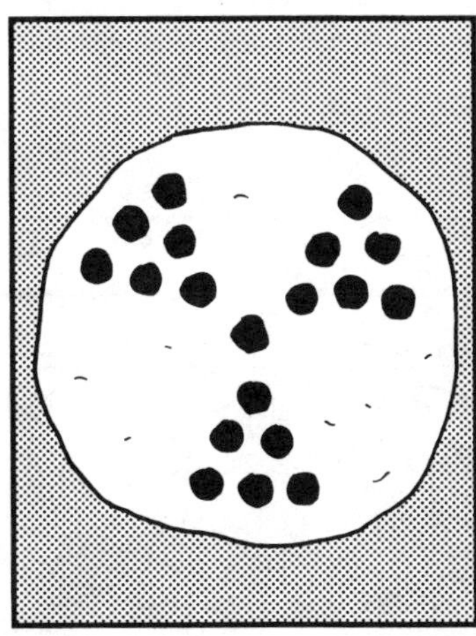

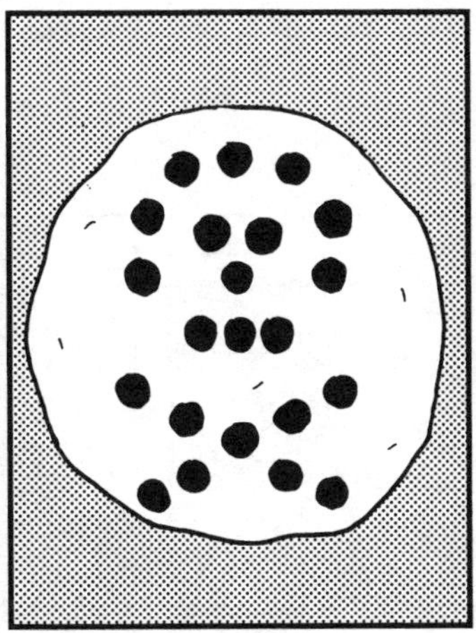

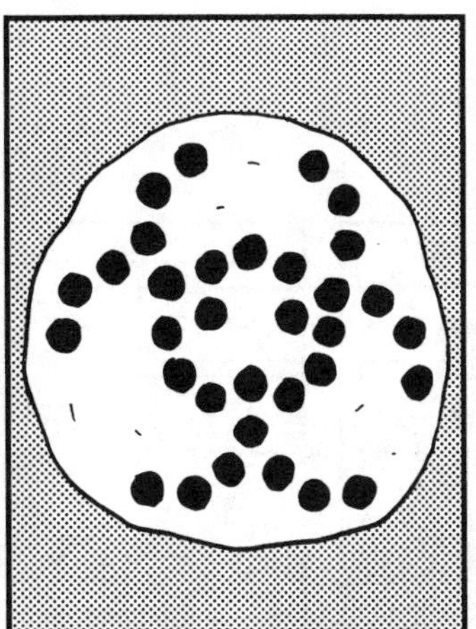

I FIGURE THIS WAY I'LL GET ALL THE COOKIES TO MYSELF.
I DUNNO. THAT BIOHAZARD ONE LOOKS PRETTY TASTY.
AMEND

HEY, THESE COOKIES YOU MADE TASTE PRETTY GOOD.
THANKS.

SERIOUSLY, WHO KNEW YOU COULD COOK SO WELL?
COOK-ING'S JUST SCIENCE, PETER.

FOR EXAMPLE, WE WERE OUT OF BROWN SUGAR, SO I SIMPLY WHIPPED UP A SUBSTITUTE USING MY JUNIOR EINSTEIN CHEMISTRY SET.
AMEND

EXCUSE ME WHILE I FIND A SINK.
THE THINGS YOU CAN DO WITH PLASTICS!

CAN I GET THIS CEREAL?
NOT IF THE FIRST INGREDIENT IS SUGAR.
WHAT ABOUT THIS ONE?
NOT IF THE FIRST INGREDIENT IS SUGAR.
CAN I GET THIS ONE? SUGAR IS THE LAST INGREDIENT.
LET ME SEE THAT.
SUGAR IS THE **ONLY** INGREDIENT, JASON!
IT'S NOT LIKE I WON'T BE ADDING MILK...
FRUCT-Os
AMEND

PETE, MY BOSS SAYS YOU HAVE TO LEAVE.
BUT IT'S ALL-YOU-CAN-EAT PIZZA NIGHT AND I'M STILL EATING!

WELL, TECHNICALLY IT'S NOW MORNING.
WHOA. I'VE BEEN HERE FOR SIX HOURS?!
AMEND

SIX HOURS, 12 MINUTES AND 37 #$*$!! SECONDS!
SIR, PLEASE. I CAN HANDLE THIS.
CAN I GET SOME TO GO?

PETER FOX, IT'S AFTER MIDNIGHT! YOU TOLD ME YOU WERE JUST GOING OUT FOR PIZZA!
I DID GO OUT FOR PIZZA.

THAT WAS OVER SIX HOURS AGO!
I WAS THERE EATING PIZZA THE WHOLE TIME! I'M NOT LYING!

ACTUALLY, I BELIEVE YOU.
YOU DO? THAT'S A FIRST.
AMEND

PAIGE, COME IN HERE!

YOU KNOW HOW I'VE BEEN STUCK AT 135 POUNDS FOREVER? WELL, LOOK AT THAT SCALE AND TELL ME WHAT IT SAYS!
AMEND

IS THIS BECAUSE YOU'RE BRAGGING, OR BECAUSE YOU CAN'T SEE IT?
A LITTLE OF BOTH.

CHECK IT OUT! I GAINED 50 POUNDS EATING PIZZA LAST NIGHT!

NOW KIDS WON'T LAUGH AT HOW SKINNY I AM WHEN I GO TO THE POOL!

TELL MOM I WENT SWIMMING.
SEAWORLD IS THAT WAY, SHAMU.
AMEND

WHY ARE YOU HANGING UPSIDE-DOWN?
I'M TRYING TO GET ALL THE WEIGHT I GAINED TO GO TO MY CHEST AND ARMS.

YOU'VE HAD SOME DUMB IDEAS BEFORE, PETER, BUT THIS MAY BE THE DUMBEST.
WE'LL JUST SEE ABOUT THAT.
AMEND

OK, IT WAS A DUMB IDEA.
YOU NEVER LISTEN.

YOU'RE SKINNY AGAIN.
TELL ME ABOUT IT. I LOST ALL 50 POUNDS OVERNIGHT.

IT'S SO UNFAIR! I EAT PIZZA AFTER PIZZA AFTER PIZZA FOR SIX HOURS STRAIGHT AND I DON'T GAIN A SINGLE LASTING POUND! I'M CURSED! CURSED, I TELL YOU!

DON'T MAKE ME CURSE YOU, SON.
EW. ARE THOSE RICE-CAKE WAFFLES?
AMEND

SHLORPH!

SKLURPF!

PBBB-
BSPT!

MOM SUGGESTED I NOT SPIT THE SEEDS AT PEOPLE.
THANK YOU, MOTHER.
WHAT'D I DO NOW?
Verlon
GLAM
AMEND

WOOHOO! I'M ALMOST THERE!
WHERE?

I'M SAVING UP TO BUY AN iPOD. THEY COST $299 AND I'VE GOT $243!
iPODS COST $299?! AND PEOPLE PAY THAT?!

ARE YOU KIDDING? PEOPLE ARE BUYING THEM LIKE CRAZY.
REALLY...

WHY DO YOU HAVE LITTLE DOLLAR SIGNS IN YOUR EYES?
IT'S, UM, JUST DIRT. DO YOU KNOW WHERE MOM HID MY SOLDERING IRON?
AMEND

WHAT ARE YOU DOING?
WORKING ON A SECRET PROJECT.

A TOP-SECRET PROJECT.

A TOP-TOP-TOP-TOP-TOP-TOP-TOP-TOP-TOP-TOP-TOP-TOP-TOP-TOP-SECRET PROJECT.
AMEND

PETER, COME BACK! DON'T YOU WANT TO HEAR WHAT IT IS?!

YOU'RE MAKING iPODS?!
I'M MAKING jPODS.

THEY'LL BE SIMILAR TO iPODS, BUT MORE ADVANCED.
AMEND

MY PLAN IS TO UNDERCUT APPLE AND SELL THEM FOR $298. I'M GOING TO BE RICH! RICH! RICH!

SO HOW ARE jPODS MORE ADVANCED?
WELL, "j" COMES AFTER "i," FOR STARTERS.

STILL WORKING ON YOUR jPOD?
IT'S COMING ALONG GREAT, PETER.

I GOT A SWEET DEAL ON SURPLUS SOUND CHIPS ON eBAY. CHECK OUT THE FIDELITY.

"ONLY MASTER YODA HAS A HIGHER MIDI-CHLORIAN COUNT!"

WERE THESE CHIPS LEFT OVER FROM "STAR WARS" TOYS?
DID I LUCK OUT, OR WHAT?!
AMEND

PRESENTING THE jPOD! BETTER THAN AN iPOD IN EVERY WAY!
SPORTO
AMEND

TWO SCROLL WHEELS IN-STEAD OF ONE! TEN BUTTONS INSTEAD OF FIVE! AND IT RUNS ON AC, SO THERE ARE NO BATTERIES TO GO DEAD!

AND BEST OF ALL, IT'S ENGINEERED TO NOT PLAY ANY BOY-BAND MUSIC.
OK, THAT MIGHT BE WORTH PAYING FOR.

OF COURSE, TECHNICALLY, IT WON'T PLAY ANY MUSIC UNLESS YOU BUY THIS ADD-ON HARD DRIVE.
WHO TORE APART MY COMPUTER?!
NO, I'LL LET YOU KEEP THAT.
SPORTO

WHAT IF I LOWERED THE PRICE TO $250?
NO!

$200?... $100?... $50?... $20?... $10?... $5?...
JASON, I DON'T WANT TO BUY YOUR STUPID jPOD!
AMEND

$1?
FINE. IT'S WORTH A DOLLAR JUST TO SHUT YOU UP.

HMM... A NEW BUSINESS MODEL...
FORGET I SAID THAT! FORGET I SAID THAT!

IT'S SAID THAT A CREATURE ROAMS THESE PARTS...

A GNARLED, FOUL-SMELLING THING WITH HOOK-LIKE CLAWS...

NOT QUITE HUMAN... NOT QUITE ANIMAL... NO ONE KNOWS FOR SURE **WHAT** IT IS...

ALL THAT'S KNOWN IS IT IS PURE EVIL. AND IT WON'T STOP LOOKING UNTIL IT FINDS...

WHY IS THERE A TENT IN MY BEDROOM?
AAAA!
THE CREATURE!
AMEND

HA HA.
PAIGE, LOOK! A SNAKE!

IT'S JUST A RUBBER SNAKE. I SAW YOU SHOWING IT TO PETER.
AMEND

NO, THIS IS THE RUBBER SNAKE I WAS SHOWING TO PETER.

AAAAAAAA!
ALWAYS BUY RUBBER SNAKES IN PAIRS.

CLICK
CLICK
CLICK
AMEND

CLICK
CLICK
CLICK
CLICK
CLICK
CLICK
CLICK

K CLICK CLICK CLICK CLICK C
LICK CLICK CLICK CLICK CLICK
K CLICK CLICK CLICK CLICK C
LICK CLICK CLICK CLICK CLICK
K CLICK CLICK CLICK CLICK C
LICK CLICK CLICK CLICK CLICK
K CLICK CLICK CLICK CLICK C
LICK CLICK CLICK CLICK CLICK
K CLICK CLICK CLICK CLICK C
LICK CLICK CLICK CLICK CLICK
K CLICK CLICK CLICK CLICK C

I DON'T KNOW WHY AMAZON BOTHERED PATENTING ONE-CLICK SHOPPING.
PAIGE, ABOUT THIS CREDIT CARD BILL.

WHAT DO YOU HAVE HIDING BEHIND THAT DOOR?
WOULDN'T YOU LIKE TO KNOW.

LESSEE...I'VE GOT A PAIR OF LEVEL TEN WARRIORS, A LEVEL FOUR WIZARD, A LEVEL TWO THIEF AND A LEVEL NINE CLERIC.

OK, I'M GOING ALL IN.
OOOO...

NO-LIMIT TEXAS D&D.
BAD NEWS. THERE'S A PAIR OF WRAITH-KINGS.
AMEND

SUNSCREEN?
THANKS.
GLAM

WHY AREN'T YOU PUTTING IT ON?
I'M WAITING FOR ONE OF THOSE CUTE BOYS OVER THERE TO OFFER TO RUB IT ON ME.
GLAM

THEY'LL NOTICE ME EVENTUALLY.

SUNBURN LOTION?
THANKS.
AMEND

YOU'RE WORK-ING ON YOUR CHRISTMAS LIST?!
I WANT TO MAKE SURE SANTA'S ELVES HAVE ENOUGH TIME.
AMEND

LAST YEAR I ASKED FOR AN IMPERIAL STAR DESTROY-ER AND WAS EXTREMELY DISAPPOINTED WHEN I DIDN'T GET ONE.

I THOUGHT SANTA GAVE YOU ONE.
HE GAVE ME A **TOY** STAR DESTROYER.

SON, CONSIDER THE DIMENSIONS OF OUR CHIMNEY.
HMM. MAYBE I SHOULD JUST GO WITH A LIGHT-SABER.

I HAD A GREAT DREAM LAST NIGHT WHERE I WAS FLYING.
ME TOO.

YOU DREAMED YOU WERE FLYING?
I DREAMED YOU WERE FLYING.

ACTUALLY, I DREAMED YOU **WERE** A FLY.

EXCUSE ME WHILE I GET A FLY **SWATTER**.
THERE WERE A BUNCH OF THOSE IN MY DREAM, TOO.
AMEND

GATES
9A, 9B, 10, 11
UM, TERRY? WE HAVE A "SITUATION."
ALL YOU SAID WAS "DON'T PACK NAIL CLIPPERS"!
NEXT VACATION WE'RE DRIVING.
SIR, I NEED YOU TO COME WITH ME...
AMEND

KIDS, IF YOU NEED TO USE THE RESTROOM, NOW'S THE TIME.
I'M OK.
I'M FINE.
I'M GOOD.

PLEASE REMAIN SEATED FOR THE NEXT HALF-HOUR AS WE BEGIN OUR APPROACH INTO WASHINGTON.
DAD? I HAVE TO GO TO THE BATHROOM.
ME TOO.
REALLY BAD.
AMEND

HI. WE HAVE A RESERVATION FOR "FOX."
TWO ROOMS. VERY GOOD.
The Senatorial

WOULD YOU PREFER THE STRUGGLING-AVERAGE-CITIZEN OR THE CORPORATE-SPECIAL-INTEREST RATE?
AMEND

WHAT'S THE DIFFERENCE?
PLEASE. THIS IS WASHINGTON.
The Senatorial

CORPORATE-SPECIAL-INTEREST.
HERE'S MY CREDIT CARD. ENJOY YOUR STAY.
The Senatorial

YOU CAN SEE THE POTOMAC FROM OUR WINDOW.
THE FOX FAMILY GOES TO WASHINGTON. WHAT A CAPITAL IDEA THIS WAS!

GET IT? GET IT? "CAPITAL IDEA"? WE'RE IN THE NATION'S CAPITAL? GET IT? GET IT?
AMEND

I GET IT, ROGER.
REALLY? YOU DIDN'T LAUGH...

WAAAAA!
PAIGE, CALM DOWN.

WAAAAA!
PAIGE, YOU'RE MAKING A SCENE.

WAAAAA!
WHAT DID YOU **EXPECT** THE NATIONAL MALL TO BE LIKE??
AMEND

SEE THAT BIG, DOMED BUILDING OVER THERE?

THAT'S THE CAPITOL BUILDING. IT'S WHERE CONGRESS MEETS TO PASS LAWS.

IT LOOKS EXACTLY LIKE THE BACK OF A $50 BILL.

I'D HEARD POLITICIANS LIKED MONEY, BUT WHOA.
NOW THAT YOU MENTION IT...
AMEND

LOOK! IT'S WOLF BLITZER!

LOOK! IT'S TED KOPPEL!

LOOK! IT'S THAT BRIT HUME GUY!
AMEND

LOOK! IT'S OUR CONGRESSMAN!
WHO?

HE WAS YOUR FATHER'S BEST FRIEND'S OLDER BROTHER.
I'M AN OLDER BROTHER...
A
AMEND

CAN I HELP YOU?
I NEED A SOUVENIR. HOW MUCH IS THE APOLLO 11 CAPSULE?
AIR & SPACE MUSEUM
GIFT SHOP

THE LITTLE WIND-UP ONES OR THE BIGGER PLASTIC REPLICAS?
THE REAL ONE OUT IN THE MUSEUM.
AMEND

AIR & SPACE MUSEUM
GIFT SHOP

LET ME GO CHECK.
WHO SAYS A GOVERNMENT IN DEBT IS ALL BAD?
AIR & SPACE MUSEUM
GIFT SHOP

IS THERE A LAW THAT SAYS THE WHITE HOUSE HAS TO BE WHITE?

I MEAN, WHAT IF THE PRESIDENT DECIDED TO PAINT IT GREEN OR BLUE OR SOMETHING COOL LIKE GLOW-IN-THE-DARK PURPLE?

WOULD THE EXECUTIVE SEAT OF POWER FOR THE UNITED STATES THEN BE CALLED "THE GLOW-IN-THE-DARK PURPLE HOUSE"?
AMEND

MY CIVICS TEACHER SKIPPED THAT LESSON.
MAYBE WE SHOULD ASK THAT HEAVILY ARMED GUARD OVER THERE.

ARE YOU REALLY WITH THE SECRET SERVICE?!
I AM.

COOL! SO DO YOU HAVE A PRIVATE TRAIN CAR AND A GUN THAT POPS OUT OF YOUR SLEEVE AND EXPLOSIVE PUTTY IN YOUR HEEL LIKE ON "WILD, WILD WEST"?!

NO, BUT I HAVE A WALKIE-TALKIE THAT WILL SUMMON 250 ARMED AGENTS, THREE HELICOPTERS AND A TANK IF THAT BALD MAN OVER THERE STEPS ANY CLOSER TO THAT FENCE.
AMEND

STEP CLOSER TO THE FENCE, DAD!
SIR, IGNORE YOUR SON, PLEASE!

I CAN'T BELIEVE I'M LOOKING AT THE ACTUAL U.S. CONSTITUTION!
YOU KNOW WHAT I CAN'T BELIEVE?
Style

THE WASHINGTON POST'S COMICS SECTION! I'VE NEVER SEEN SUCH A GREAT COMICS SECTION BEFORE!
Style

WHOEVER IS IN CHARGE OF THEIR COMICS IS A GENIUS! NO, A SUPER-GENIUS! THEY SHOULD RUN THE WHOLE PAPER!
Style
AMEND

I'D ROLL MY EYES, BUT SOMETHING TELLS ME I SHOULDN'T.
I HEAR THEY PAY SOME OF THE CARTOON-ISTS REALLY WELL, TOO.
Style

PAIGE, LET'S GO! WE NEED TO GET TO THE AIRPORT!
DO WE HAVE TO?
CAN'T WE STAY IN WASHINGTON A LITTLE LONGER?
The Senatorial
AMEND
YOU KIDS ARE INCREDIBLE! JUST YESTERDAY YOU WERE DYING TO GO HOME!
WHAT'S CHANGED?
IT WASN'T 6:00 A.M. THEN.

MY CLASSES ARE ALL OVER THE SCHOOL. I KEEP GETTING LOST.
I HAVE A GPS WRIST-WATCH. I CAN'T GET LOST.
I UPLOADED A MAP OF THE ENTIRE CAMPUS. IT'S QUITE USEFUL.
FOR EXAMPLE, IT'S SHOWING MY MATH CLASSROOM IS 108.3 METERS THAT WAY.
MY SCIENCE CLASS IS 92.7 METERS THAT WAY.
AMEND
AND TWO HOT CHICKS ARE SITTING 1.1 METERS TO MY RIGHT.
GET LOST, MORTON.
REALLY LOST.
HELLO? WEREN'T YOU LISTENING?

SHOULDN'T YOU BE UPSTAIRS DOING HOMEWORK?
MOTHER, PLEASE.

IT'S THE SECOND WEEK OF SCHOOL. I DON'T HAVE ANY HOMEWORK.
AMEND

BECAUSE YOU HAVEN'T BEEN ASSIGNED ANY, OR BECAUSE YOU'VE ALREADY FINISHED IT FOR THE YEAR?
I SUPPOSE I COULD QUINTUPLE-CHECK MY ANSWERS AGAIN...

I HOLD IN MY HAND AN ORDINARY PAPER BAG INTO WHICH WAS PLACED A PEANUT BUTTER AND SPINACH SANDWICH BY MY MOTHER.
AMEND

HOWEVER, WHEN I REACH INTO IT, I NOW PRODUCE... ALAKAZAM!

A PEANUT BUTTER AND SPINACH SANDWICH.
DAVID COPPERFIELD HAS IT SO GOOD.

WHAT'S THAT YOU'RE READING?
THE NEW YORK TIMES.

THEY HAVE AN OFFLINE EDITION?
YES, AND DON'T MAKE ME WHACK YOU WITH IT.
AMEND

HERE'S YOUR HELMET.
WHAT'S THIS FOR?

THE NFL SEASON KICKS OFF ON TV TONIGHT.
IT'S NOT THE SUPER BOWL. WE CAN WATCH THE GAME WITHOUT DRESSING UP, PETER.

PAIGE CLAIMS SHE HAS DIBS ON THE TV.
HMM. WE MIGHT NEED SOME SHOULDER PADS, TOO, THEN.
AMEND

Which is larger? A liter of Pepsi or a quart of Pepsi?

"Carbonation" refers to the process by which what is added to a soda?
a. Carbon monoxide, b. Carbon fibers, c. Carbon dioxide
AMEND

SIR, ABOUT THIS POP QUIZ...
QUESTION SEVEN HAS A TYPO, PEOPLE. IT SHOULD SAY — "DIET COKE."

PICK A CARD, ANY CARD.

LET'S SEE... MY PSYCHIC POWERS TELL ME THE CARD YOU'VE CHOSEN IS BLUE AND GRAY AND SAYS "UNIVERSAL CASINOS." AM I RIGHT?

HA HA! I AM RIGHT, AREN'T I!
DINGUS, YOU'RE HOLDING THE DECK UPSIDE-DOWN.
AMEND

BRB brb BRB brb BRB brb BRB
brb BRB brb BRB brb BRB brb
BRB brb BRB brb BRB brb BRB

:-);-):-);-):-);-):-)
;-):-);-):-);-):-);-)
:-);-):-);-):-);-):-)

<g><G><g><G><g><G><g>
<G><g><G><g><G><g><G>
<g><G><g><G><g><G><g>

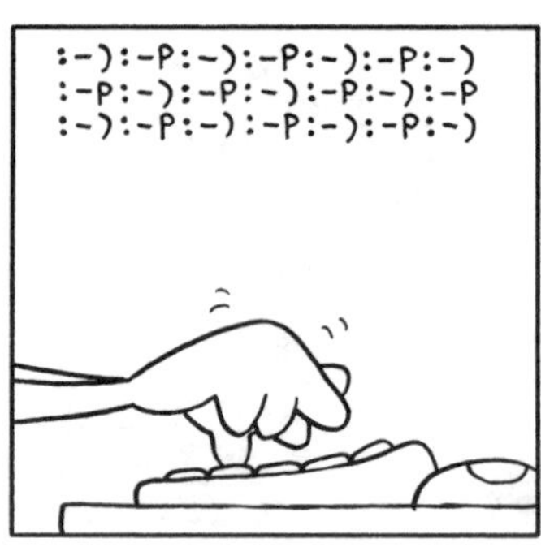
:-):-P:-):-P:-):-P:-)
:-P:-):-P:-):-P:-):-P
:-):-P:-):-P:-):-P:-)

AFKafkAFKafkAFKafkAFK
afkAFKafkAFKafkAFKafk
AFKafkAFKafkAFKafkAFK
AMEND

>:0>:o>:0>:o>:0>:o>:0
>:o>:0>:o>:0>:o>:0>:o
>:0>:o>:0>:o>:0>:o>:0

I HAD NO IDEA TYPING CLASS WOULD BE SO PRACTICAL!
OK, EVERYONE, FINGERS ON THE "R," "O," "T," "F," AND "L" KEYS NOW...

HELLO. YOU'VE REACHED THE FOX RESIDENCE.
AMEND

PLEASE LEAVE A MESSAGE AFTER THE BEEP.

...UNLESS YOU'RE A BOY CALLING TO ASK PAIGE OUT FOR A DATE, IN WHICH CASE, PLEASE HANG UP AND DIAL 555-6750.

SHE HAS HER OWN PHONE?
IT'S THE LOCAL PSYCH WARD.

HOW'S YOUR HOMEWORK COMING ALONG?
PRETTY WELL.
THYME

I READ THE FIRST SENTENCE OF THE NOVEL I'M SUPPOSED TO HAVE FINISHED BY TOMORROW.

ALL RIGHT, PAIGE! WAY TO GO!
THYME
AMEND

IT'S SO NICE TO FOLLOW IN YOUR FOOTSTEPS.
PAIGE, QUIET. I'M TAKING MY PRE-HOMEWORK NAP PRE-NAP.
A

WHO LET THE IGUANA OUT? WHO! WHO! WHOO! WHO!

WHO LET THE IGUANA OUT? WHO! WHO! WHOO! WHO!

WHO LET THE—
IT'S "WHO LET THE DOGS OUT," DIMWIT.
A
GLAM

ARE YOU SURE?
AAAAA! MOTHERRR!
AMEND

I THINK THEY'VE FINALLY FOUND A WAY TO MAKE US STUDY.
WE ALSO HAVE π/3 RADIANS PIZZA SLICES.
Today's Special
$(\frac{1}{256})^{\frac{1}{4}}$ lb. burger
avec pommes frites
and a
473.176cc drink
$\$ \ln e^{3.99}$
A
AMEND

I WAS LOOKING AT YOU IN MATH CLASS AND NOTICED YOU WERE WRITHING IN AGONY.

IF YOU FIND THE SUBJECT DIFFICULT, I'D BE HAPPY TO TUTOR YOU.
AMEND

ONE-ON-ONE? MY PLACE? SAY, 4:30-ISH? I'LL HAVE MOTHER CHILL THE ROOT BEER.

I WAS WRITHING IN AGONY **BECAUSE** YOU WERE LOOKING AT ME.
I'LL LET YOU USE MY NEW CALCU-LATOR...

ARE YOU GOING TO THE FOOTBALL GAME TONIGHT?
NAH.

EVER SINCE I TRIED OUT FOR THE TEAM LAST YEAR IT'S BEEN TOO PAINFUL TO WATCH THEM PLAY.
AMEND

BECAUSE YOU AREN'T OUT THERE WITH THEM?
BECAUSE THE COACH THROWS HIS CLIPBOARD AT ME.

DO YOU SELL ULTRAVIOLET BULL?
EXCUSE ME?
WHAT ABOUT REGULAR VIOLET BULL?
NO.
BLUE BULL?
NO.
GREEN BULL?
NO.
YELLOW BULL?
NO.
ORANGE BULL?
NO.
Windows CR™
Press any key to continue
RATS. OK, I'LL TAKE A RED BULL.
I WAS HOPING FOR SOMETHING A LITTLE HIGHER-ENERGY.
AT LEAST IT ISN'T **INFRARED** BULL.
AMEND

THERE'S A BOX FULL OF DRESSES AND THINGS BY THE BACK DOOR.
I KNOW.

I CLEANED OUT MY CLOSET TODAY. THOSE ARE FOR CHARITY.

AH.

CHARITY BEGINS AT HOME, RIGHT?...
AMEND

HELLO, YOUNG MAN. I'M QUINCY'S MOTHER.

I DECIDED TO DROP BY TO SEE HOW HIS ADOPTED FAMILY IS TREATING HIM.

JASON, IF YOU DON'T MIND, I'M IN THE MIDDLE OF WRITING A FIVE-PAGE PAPER FOR SCHOOL TOMORROW.
AMEND

COULD YOU MAKE IT SIX PAGES? MY LITTLE QUINCYKINS NEEDS FATTENING UP.
IF THIS ESSAY DISAPPEARS, PAL...

HELLO.
YOU MUST
BE PAIGE.

MY SON QUINCY HAS TOLD
ME ALL ABOUT YOU. VERY
FLATTERING THINGS, I
MIGHT ADD.
AMEND

JASON,
GO AWAY.

MMM. YOUR
BREATH
DOES SMELL
LIKE FRESH
MEALWORMS!
I SAID
GO
AWAY!

SO WHEN CAN
I EXPECT TO
SEE GRAND-
CHILDREN?
WHAT?!

MY SON TELLS ME THE
TWO OF YOU ARE PLAN-
NING TO GET MARRIED.
WE ARE
NOT!
AMEND

OH, DEAR.
DID MY LITTLE
QUINCYWOO
TELL ME A
FIB?

WELL, IF THE
TWO OF YOU
WANT TO
CANOODLE
IN SIN, THAT'S
YOUR CHOICE.
THE QUES-
TION IS, WILL
IT BE A SIN
WHEN I KILL
YOU?!

ICKERDOODLES! WHAT IS THAT STENCH?!
I'M COOKING DINNER.

IT'S STEWED BELL PEPPERS STUFFED WITH DICED EGGPLANT.

YOU DON'T EXPECT MY SWEET LITTLE QUINCY TO EAT THAT, DO YOU?!
NO, BUT I EXPECT MY CHILDREN TO.

MAYBE YOU SHOULD TRY MY RECIPE FOR STEWED CRICKETS. THEY MIGHT LIKE THAT BETTER.
OUT!
AMEND

MY QUINCY DIDN'T TELL ME THERE WERE OTHER IGUANAS HERE!
WHAT ON EARTH ARE YOU TALK-ING ABOUT?
GOLFSTER

YOU. YOU'RE AN IGUANA, AREN'T YOU?
OF COURSE I'M NOT AN IGUANA.
GOLFSTER

THEN WHAT KIND OF REPTILE ARE YOU?
I'M NOT A REPTILE. I'M A MAMMAL.
GOLFSTER

DON'T BE SILLY. MAMMALS HAVE HAIR.
OK, JASON! GAME'S OVER!

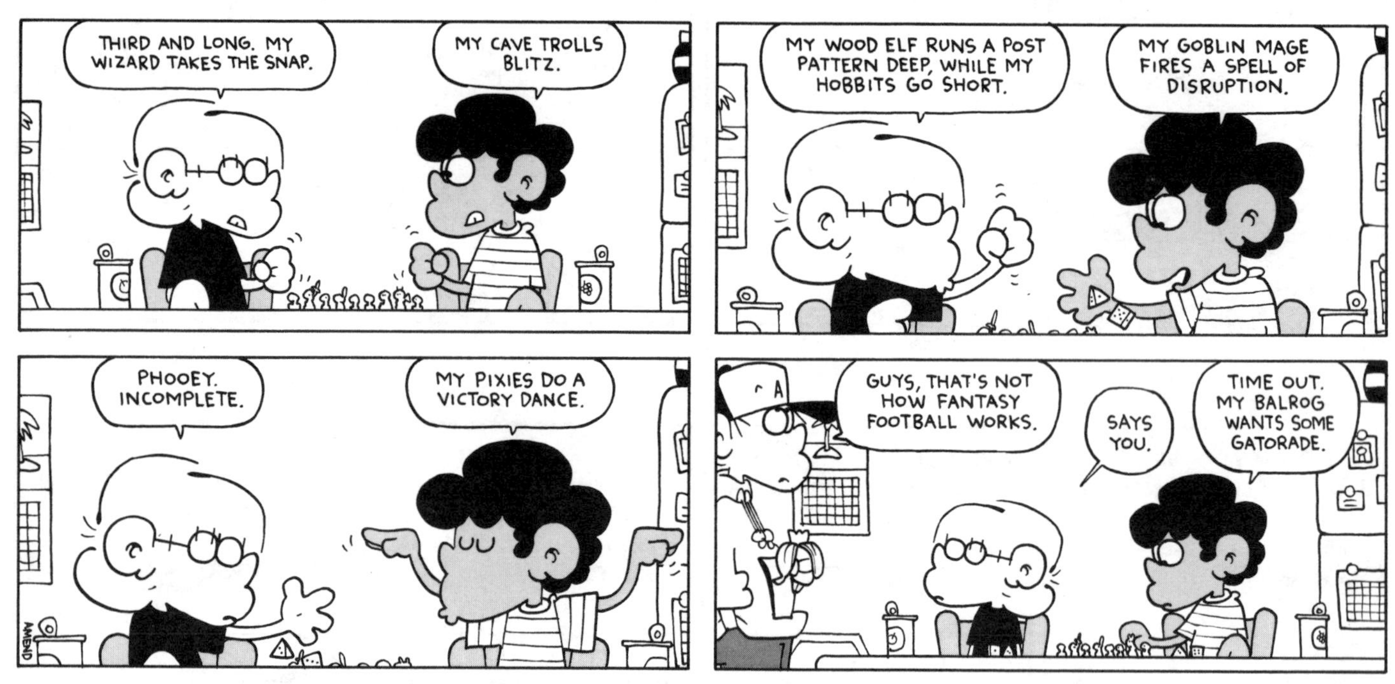
THIRD AND LONG. MY WIZARD TAKES THE SNAP.
MY CAVE TROLLS BLITZ.
MY WOOD ELF RUNS A POST PATTERN DEEP, WHILE MY HOBBITS GO SHORT.
MY GOBLIN MAGE FIRES A SPELL OF DISRUPTION.
PHOOEY. INCOMPLETE.
MY PIXIES DO A VICTORY DANCE.
AMEND
GUYS, THAT'S NOT HOW FANTASY FOOTBALL WORKS.
SAYS YOU.
TIME OUT. MY BALROG WANTS SOME GATORADE.

G'DAY, MATE!
WHAT?

I'M WORKING ON MY AUSTRALIAN ACCENT.
IT'S NOT VERY CONVINCING.
AMEND

HOLD ON. LET ME TRY AGAIN.

G'DAY, MATE!
MUCH BETTER.

MRS. JOHNSTON CALLED, PETER. SHE SAYS SHE SAW YOU DRIVING LIKE A MANIAC ON PINE STREET AFTER SCHOOL.
THAT'S NOT TRUE!

SHE'S MISTAKEN! SHE MUST'VE SEEN SOMEONE ELSE!
AMEND

YOU'RE SURE?
I SWEAR!

OK.
NOW IF SHE'D SAID **MAPLE** STREET...
THYME

THIS IS SEAN HANNITY, REMINDING YOU TO BUY MY NEW BOOK.
AND THIS IS ALAN COLMES, REMINDING YOU TO BUY MY NEW BOOK.

OUR GUEST THIS EVENING IS FELLOW FOX NEWS HOST NEIL CAVUTO, WHO'S GOING TO REMIND US TO BUY HIS NEW BOOK.
AMEND

BUT BEFORE WE GET TO THAT, LET'S CHECK IN WITH BILL O'REILLY FOR A PREVIEW OF TONIGHT'S "O'REILLY FACTOR"...

I HAVE A NEW BOOK, FOLKS.
JASON, YOUR IGUANA THREW UP ON THE SOFA AGAIN...

I NEED TO USE THE COMPUTER.
HOLD ON. I'M IN THE MIDDLE OF PLAYING ALIEN ARMAGEDDON.

JASON, I HAVE TO WRITE A BOOK REPORT!
AND I HAVE TO SAVE THE RESIDENTS OF EARTH FROM MASS EXTERMINATION!
AMEND

I KNOW. HOW ABOUT I DON'T SAVE YOUR ENGLISH TEACHER?

SHEESH. TRY TO OFFER SOMEONE A REASONABLE COMPROMISE...

I ALWAYS FORGET MY LOCKER COMBINATION.
DO WHAT I DO.

I ASSOCIATE EACH NUMBER WITH SOMETHING EASY TO REMEMBER.

MINE IS THE ATOMIC NUMBER OF CARBON LEFT, THE ATOMIC NUMBER OF PHOSPHORUS RIGHT, AND THE ATOMIC NUMBER OF MANGANESE LEFT.

I ALSO ALWAYS FORGET NOT TO DISCUSS THESE THINGS WITH YOU.
LAST YEAR I HAD KRYPTON.
AMEND

ONE-AND-THREE IN THE PRESEASON MEANS NOTHING. I REPEAT, NOTHING.

I GOT TWO WORDS FOR YOU: MARSHALL FAULK. I GOT ANOTHER TWO: ISAAC BRUCE.

WE'RE GOING ALL THE WAY, BABY! I CAN FEEL IT! I CAN FEEL IT!

MOM, THE RAM YOU INSTALLED WASN'T FROM ST. LOUIS, BY ANY CHANCE?
THE SEAHAWKS ARE OVER-RATED. TRUST ME.
AMEND

THIS WILL BE A 51-YARD FIELD GOAL ATTEMPT.

VAN PELT TO HOLD, BROWN TO KICK. HERE'S THE SNAP...

AND VAN PELT PULLS THE BALL AWAY AT THE LAST SECOND!

BROWN KICKS NOTHING BUT AIR! HE'S FLAT ON HIS BACK!

VAN PELT IS LAUGHING! THE GAME IS OVER! WHAT AN ENDING!
AMEND

I GUESS THE SNOOPY BLIMPS WERE JUST THE BEGINNING.
TODAY'S NFL COVERAGE HAS BEEN BROUGHT TO YOU BY METLIFE...

ASK ME WHAT THE DATE IS.
WHAT'S THE DATE?

10-4, GOOD BUDDY.
AMEND

GET IT?! GET IT?! IT'S A CB-RADIO JOKE!
NOW TELL ME WHAT THE YEAR IS.

WHY?
BECAUSE I'M CURIOUS IF YOU KNOW.

A... B... C... D... E... F...

G... H... I... J...

HEY, THERE'S NO "K."
AMEND

DO YOU STILL HAVE THE RECEIPT FOR THIS ALPHABET SOUP, MOM?
I'M NOT RETURNING ANOTHER CAN, JASON.

"COUNTER-STRIKE" HAS A CHEAT CODE FOR INVULNERABILITY.

"UNREAL TOURNAMENT" HAS A CHEAT CODE FOR INVULNERABILITY.

"DOOM 3" HAS A CHEAT CODE FOR INVULNERABILITY.

BUT A SIMPLE GAME LIKE DODGEBALL?! NOOOOOO...
AMEND

SO THESE COMPUTER EXPERTS DEMONSTRATED HOW A TRAINED CHIMP COULD HACK THE SOFT-WARE THAT TABULATES ELECTRONIC VOTING.
THYME

MAKES YOU WONDER IF WE SHOULDN'T JUST STICK WITH SOMETHING SIMPLE AND REVIEWABLE LIKE PAPER BALLOTS.
AMEND

THYME

THEN AGAIN, HAVING SOME MONKEY ELECTED PRESIDENT MIGHT BE KINDA FUNNY.
WE COULD DO WORSE.
THYME

WANT THE PAPER DOLLS I MADE?
WHY WOULD I WANT PAPER DOLLS?!

SHEESH, EILEEN! DO YOU THINK I'M SOME SORT OF DWEEB?!
AMEND

I MESSED UP. THEY CAME OUT LOOKING LIKE TWO-HEADED ALIENS.

NOW ABOUT THE QUESTION YOU POSED...
HEY, MARCUS! LOOK WHAT I GOT!

ISN'T PETER SUPPOSED TO BE HELPING US?
YES.

HE'S INSIDE WATCHING SOME SILLY FOOTBALL GAME THAT'S TIED IN THE FOURTH QUARTER.
AMEND

TEXAS-OKLAHOMA??
SOMETHING LIKE THAT.

AREN'T DADDY AND PETER SUPPOSED TO BE HELPING YOU?
YES.

YOU WERE RIGHT, MOM! DOING YOGA **IS** FUN!
MY RETORT WILL COMMENCE AS SOON AS I CAN TOUCH MY TOES.
AMEND

STEVE'S HOUSE HAS A 60-INCH WIDESCREEN HIGH-DEF TV.
GOOD FOR STEVE.
ATLANTIC

WITH 7.1 SURROUND SOUND AND A 500-DISC DVD CAROUSEL WITH EVERY ACTION FLICK EVER MADE.
GOOD FOR STEVE.
AMEND

AND AN XBOX AND A PS2 AND A GAME-CUBE THAT HE CAN PLAY WHENEVER HE WANTS.
GOOD FOR STEVE.

WHY CAN'T THERE EVER BE GOOD FOR PETER?!
BECAUSE I WANT **BETTER** FOR PETER.
NEXT, ON THE WIDE WORLD OF DICKENS...
INDIAN

DOES THIS SCREENSAVER MAKE ME LOOK FAT?
AMEND

BE HONEST. I CAN TAKE IT.

WAAA! IT DOES! I CAN TELL BY THE WAY YOU'RE LOOKING AT ME!

THE NEW THIN iFRUIT MODELS ARE MAKING HIM SELF-CONSCIOUS.
IT'S NOT **MY** FAULT I'M BIG-CHIPPED!

PAIGE, ARE YOU ALL RIGHT? YOU LOOK AWFUL.
I THINK I'M SICK.

POOR THING. YOU GO BACK TO BED, I'LL CALL THE SCHOOL. THERE MUST BE A BUG GOING AROUND.

JASON'S STAYING HOME SICK TODAY, ALSO.
AMEND

MISS FOX, ARE YOU ALL RIGHT? YOU LOOK AWFUL.
I'M FINE. REALLY.

PETER, THANK GOODNESS YOU ANSWERED.
MOM, WHAT'S WRONG?

I HAVE TO BE SOME-WHERE IN 10 MINUTES AND I NEED THE CAR.
I'M ON MY WAY HOME. I JUST PULLED ONTO ELM STREET.
AMEND

ELM STREET??

PETER, HOW MANY TIMES DO I HAVE TO TELL YOU NOT TO TALK ON THE PHONE WHILE DRIVING?!
WON'T HAP-PEN AGAIN.

NOW LET'S CHECK THE CHICKEN WE PUT IN THE OVEN... YIKES, WE'VE BURNED IT.

NOW LET'S GIVE THE PASTA A QUICK STIR... UH-OH, THIS ISN'T HOW IT'S SUPPOSED TO LOOK.

NOW LET'S SEE HOW OUR VEGETABLES ARE... EEK! WHERE'S THAT FIRE EXTINGUISHER?

FINALLY, A COOKING SHOW I CAN RELATE TO.
NOW LET'S LOOK UP "PIZZA DELIVERY" IN THE PHONE BOOK...
AMEND

THE FOUR-HOUR "FARSCAPE" MINISERIES STARTS TOMORROW!
WHAT'S "FARSCAPE"?

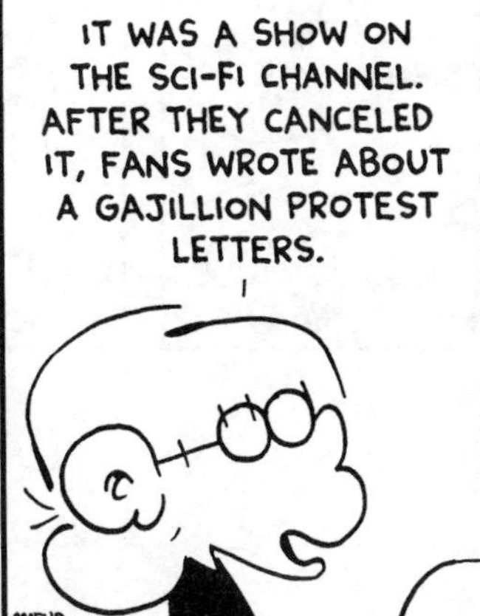
IT WAS A SHOW ON THE SCI-FI CHANNEL. AFTER THEY CANCELED IT, FANS WROTE ABOUT A GAJILLION PROTEST LETTERS.
AMEND

TOTAL, OR EACH?

WELL, I CAN ONLY SPEAK FOR MYSELF...
IS THIS WHY I COULDN'T FIND A STAMP FOR SIX MONTHS?

OK, HERE'S THE PLAY...

GO 40 YARDS DOWNFIELD, THEN TURN LEFT AND GO 20 YARDS.

THEN TURN RIGHT AND GO 25 YARDS, THEN TURN RIGHT AGAIN AND GO 30 YARDS.
30
25
20
40
Start

THEN TURN RIGHT AND GO 30 YARDS, THEN TURN LEFT AND GO 10 YARDS.

THEN TURN LEFT AND GO 15 YARDS, THEN TURN LEFT AND GO 20 YARDS, THEN TURN LEFT AND GO 50 YARDS AND I'LL HIT YOU WITH THE BALL.

AMEND

WON'T I BE RIGHT BACK WHERE I STARTED?
I CAN'T THROW VERY FAR.

OK, HERE'S THE **NEW** PLAY...
I NEVER GET TO BE QUARTERBACK.

I NEED YOU TO SIGN OFF ON MY PHYS-ED HOMEWORK.

THIS SAYS YOU'RE SUPPOSED TO DO 100 SIT-UPS. YOU REALLY DID THAT MANY?

I DID FOUR.
FOUR ISN'T 100, JASON.

ALLOW ME TO EXPLAIN THE CONCEPT OF BINARY NUMBERS.
ALLOW ME TO EXPLAIN THE TERM "FAT CHANCE."
AMEND

PETER, WHY ARE THE LEAVES NOT RAKED?
IT'S DAD'S FAULT.

HOW'S THAT?
HE ONLY ASKED ME ONE TIME TO DO IT. EVERYONE KNOWS I NEED TO BE TOLD FIVE OR SIX TIMES BEFORE I'LL DO ANYTHING.

FINE. GET OUT THERE. GET OUT THERE. GET OUT THERE. GET OUT THERE.
THAT ONLY COUNTS AS FOUR. DAD'S EXPIRED.

GET OUT THERE!
OK! SHEESH! YOU DON'T HAVE TO YELL!
AMEND

HAVE YOU SEEN THE UPDATED PLAYSTATION-2? IT'S SUPER SLIM.
GOLFY

IT'D LOOK GREAT ON TOP OF OUR TV. HINT HINT HINT.
HAVE YOU SEEN THIS?

IT'S EVEN SLIMMER.
GOLFY

HINT HINT HINT.
I NEVER SHOULD HAVE GIVEN HIM THAT WALLET FOR HIS BIRTHDAY.
AMEND

THIS BOOK REPORT I'M DOING HAS ME STUMPED.
A

I'M TOTALLY AT A LOSS WHERE TO GO WITH IT.
AMEND

I'VE NEVER DONE ONE LIKE THIS.
WHAT'S DIFFERENT?
A

I'VE ACTUALLY READ THE BOOK.
WHOA. THAT **WOULD** BE WEIRD.
A

CHECK IT OUT— PAIGE LEFT HER DIARY WHERE I COULD FIND IT!
WHAT'S IT SAY? WHAT'S IT SAY?
AMEND

"DEAR DIARY, TODAY I'M LEAVING MY DIARY WHERE JASON CAN FIND IT SO I CAN BEAT HIM UP WHEN I CATCH HIM READING IT."
DIARY

WELL, WELL, WHAT HAVE WE HERE?

I NEED TO GET BETTER AT SMELLING HER SET-UPS.
I DON'T EVEN WANT TO KNOW WHAT I'M SMELLING RIGHT NOW.

OOF!

OOF!
AMEND

OOF!

MAYBE IT NEEDS BATTERIES.
DID IT COME WITH A MANUAL?

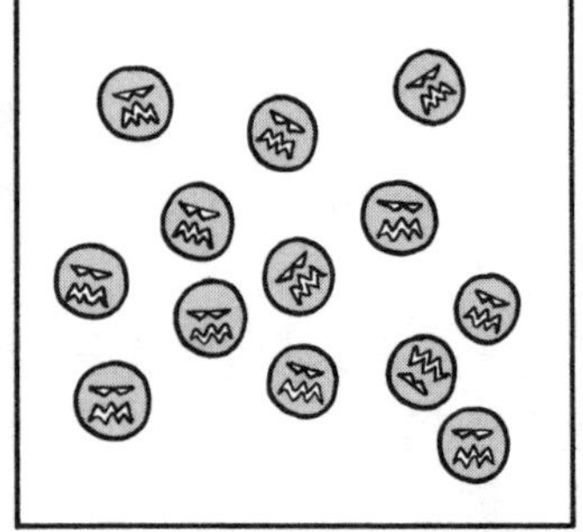

PUMPKINS AREN'T THE ONLY SCARY VEGETABLES.
WHO CARVED A FACE IN THE TOFU?!
A
AMEND

SWEET.

HEY, PETER, I LIKE HOW YOUR PUMPKIN TURNED OUT. NICE JOB!
AMEND

I HAVEN'T CARVED MINE YET. THAT'S PAIGE'S PUMPKIN.

YOUR PUMPKIN IS PATHETIC.
MY **PUMPKIN** IS?

MOM, CAN WE HAVE SPINACH WITH DINNER SOMETIME THIS WEEK?
I WAS PLANNING ON IT FOR TONIGHT, ACTUALLY.

GOOD. MAKE A LOT OF IT, PLEASE.
I DIDN'T KNOW YOU LIKED IT SO MUCH.
AMEND

I DON'T. I NEED IT FOR MY SWAMP THING COSTUME.
IN THAT CASE, WE **WON'T** BE HAVING SPINACH THIS WEEK.

WORKED LIKE A CHARM.
EXCELLENT. NOW GO ASK FOR BROCCOLI.

OK, HOW'S THIS FOR A COSTUME IDEA...

I DRESS UP LIKE AN EIGHT-YEAR-OLD.
AMEND

THEN I PUT ON A WITCH'S OUTFIT.

JUST ACCEPT IT, PAIGE, YOU'RE TOO OLD FOR TRICK-OR-TREATING.
NOOOOO!

MOM, IS IT OK TO DECORATE THE FRONT HALL WITH SPIDERWEBS?
THAT'S FINE.

THEY HAD SOME PRETTY REALISTIC WEBS ON SALE AT THE DRUGSTORE. IS THAT WHAT YOU'RE USING?
AMEND

NO. THOSE WERE TOO EXPENSIVE.
THEN WHAT ARE YOU USING?

GET TO WORK, LITTLE FELLAS.
I SAID, WHAT ARE YOU USING?

THE POOR KID IS TRICK-OR-TREATING AND EVERYONE KEEPS GIVING HIM ROCKS!
A

YOU KNOW WHAT HE SHOULD DO? HE SHOULD EAT THE ROCKS AND SAY HE NATURALLY ASSUMED THEY WERE CANDY.
A

THEN WHEN HE REQUIRES EMERGENCY SURGERY FOR A BLOCKED INTESTINE, HE CAN SUE ALL THE NEIGHBORS FOR EVERY PENNY THEY'VE GOT.
AMEND

FORTUNATELY, CARTOON CHARACTERS DON'T THINK THE WAY YOU DO.
"IT'S THE GREAT LAWSUIT, CHARLIE BROWN!"
A

DON'T WALK OVER THERE. WALK OVER HERE.
YEAH, RIGHT.

EVERY HALLOWEEN IT'S THE SAME THING, JASON— YOU BOOBY-TRAP OUR YARD WITH POP-UP ZOMBIES AND FAKE BATS THAT FALL OUT OF THE TREES.
AMEND

YOU JUST WANT ME TO STEP ON SOME STUPID TRIP WIRE.

I WAS JUST WARNING YOU ABOUT THE DOG D—
AAAA! MY NEW SHOES!

MY PARTY JUST STARTED! WHO ATE ALL THE POPCORN?!

AND THE BROWNIES?!

AND THE APPLES I BROUGHT FOR BOBBING?!

AND FINISHED ALL THE PUNCH?!

WHY'S EVERYONE LOOKING AT ME?
AMEND